Journey Through the Mandalas

Welcome

'Exploring Mandalas Coloring Book for the Mind and Soul'

Embark on a transformative journey through 50 pages of intricate designs, each carefully crafted to evoke a sense of calm and introspection. Delve into the mesmerizing world of mandalas as you color your way through this immersive experience. Let the rhythmic strokes of your coloring utensils guide you to a place of inner peace and mindfulness. Whether you're seeking relaxation, inspiration, or simply a moment of creative expression, this book offers a sanctuary for your spirit to wander and explore.

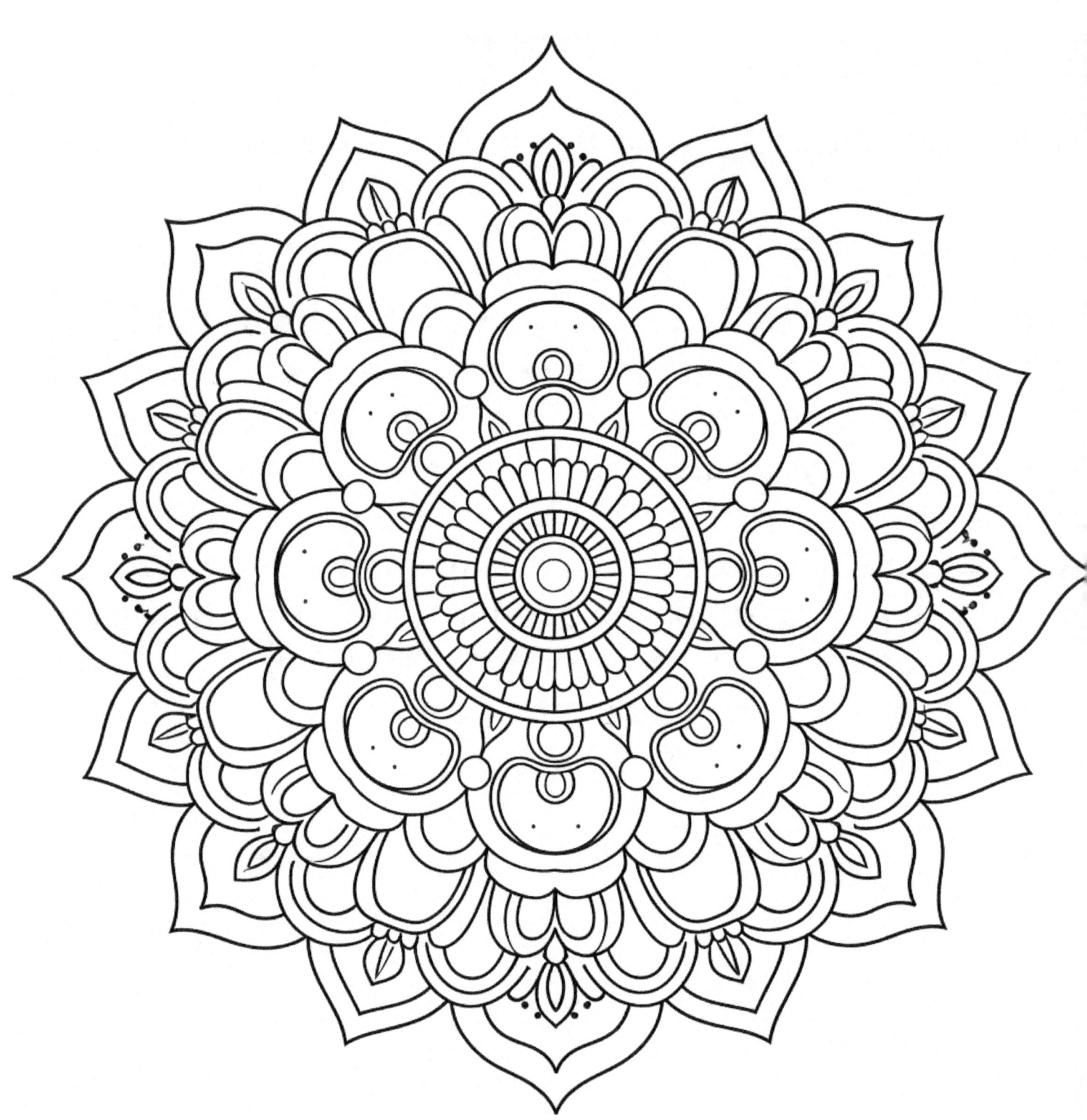

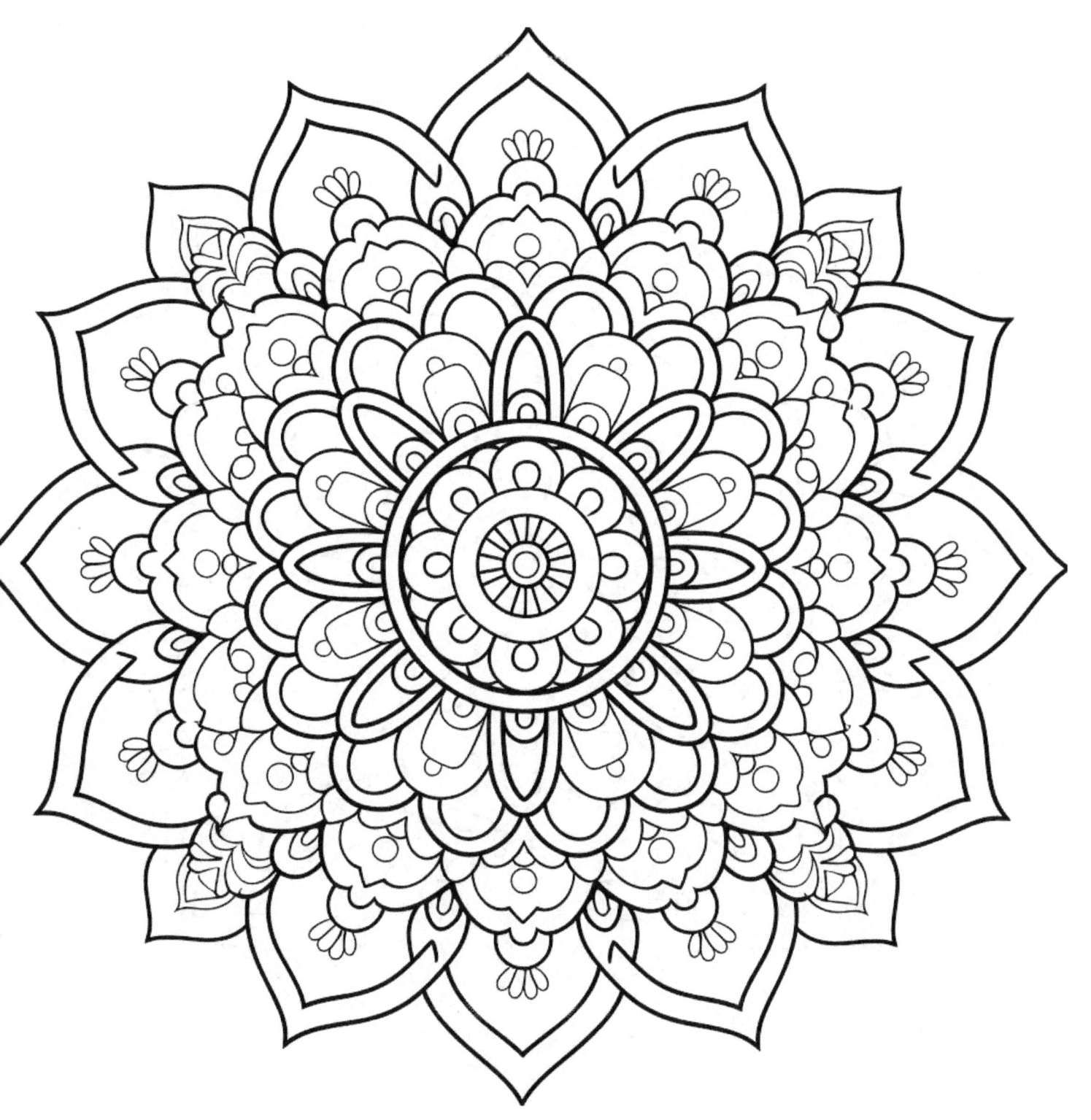

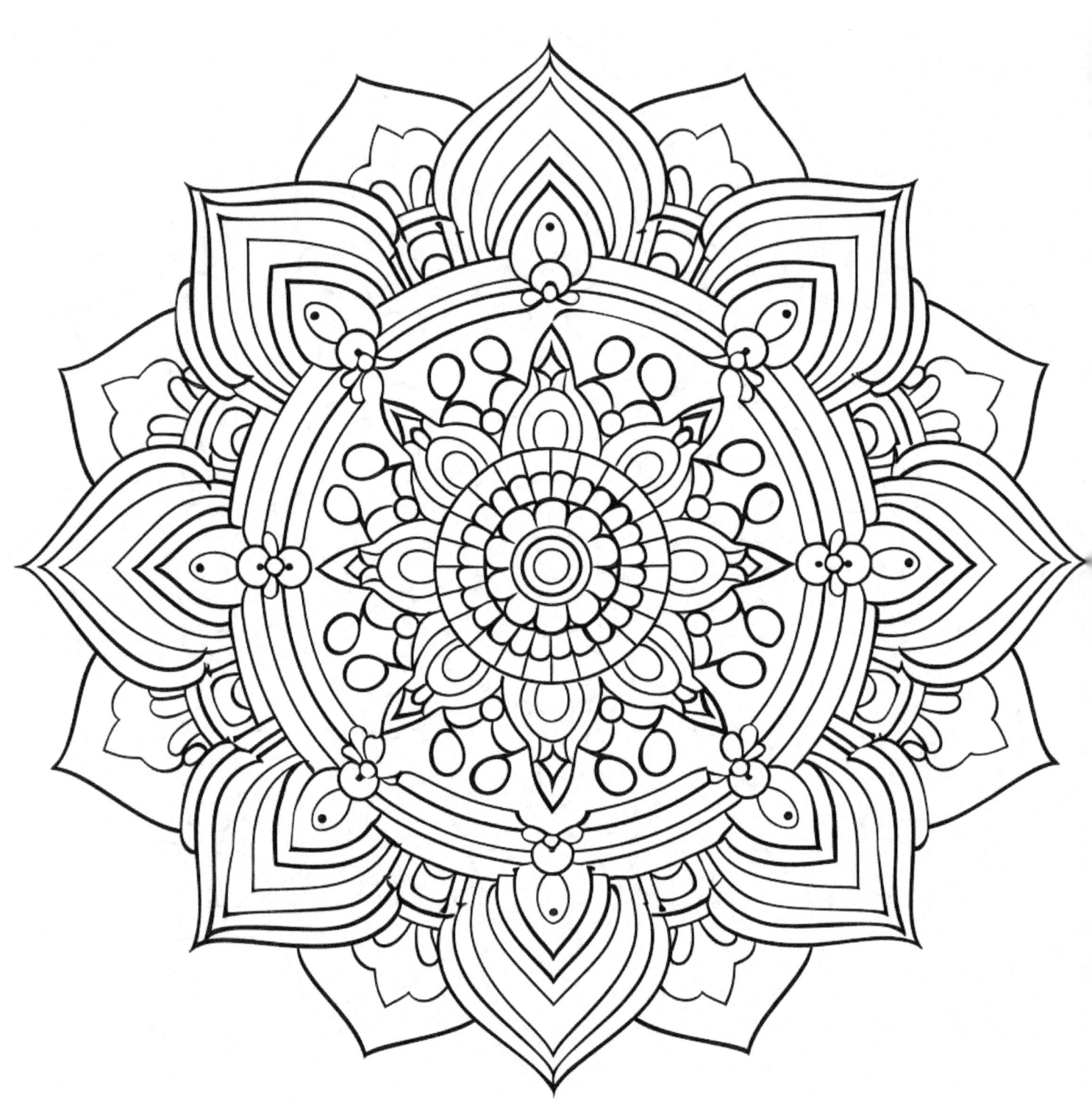

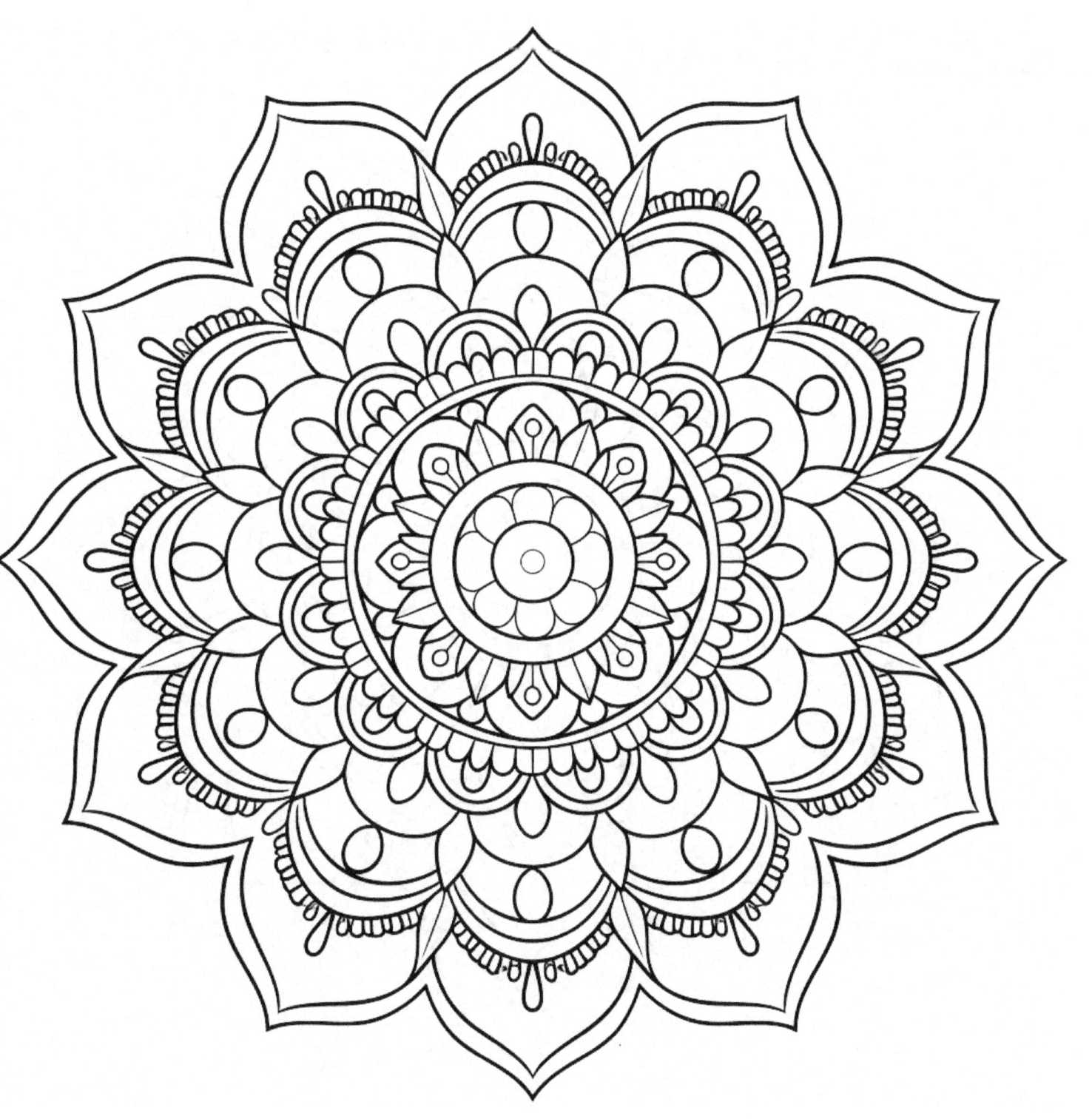

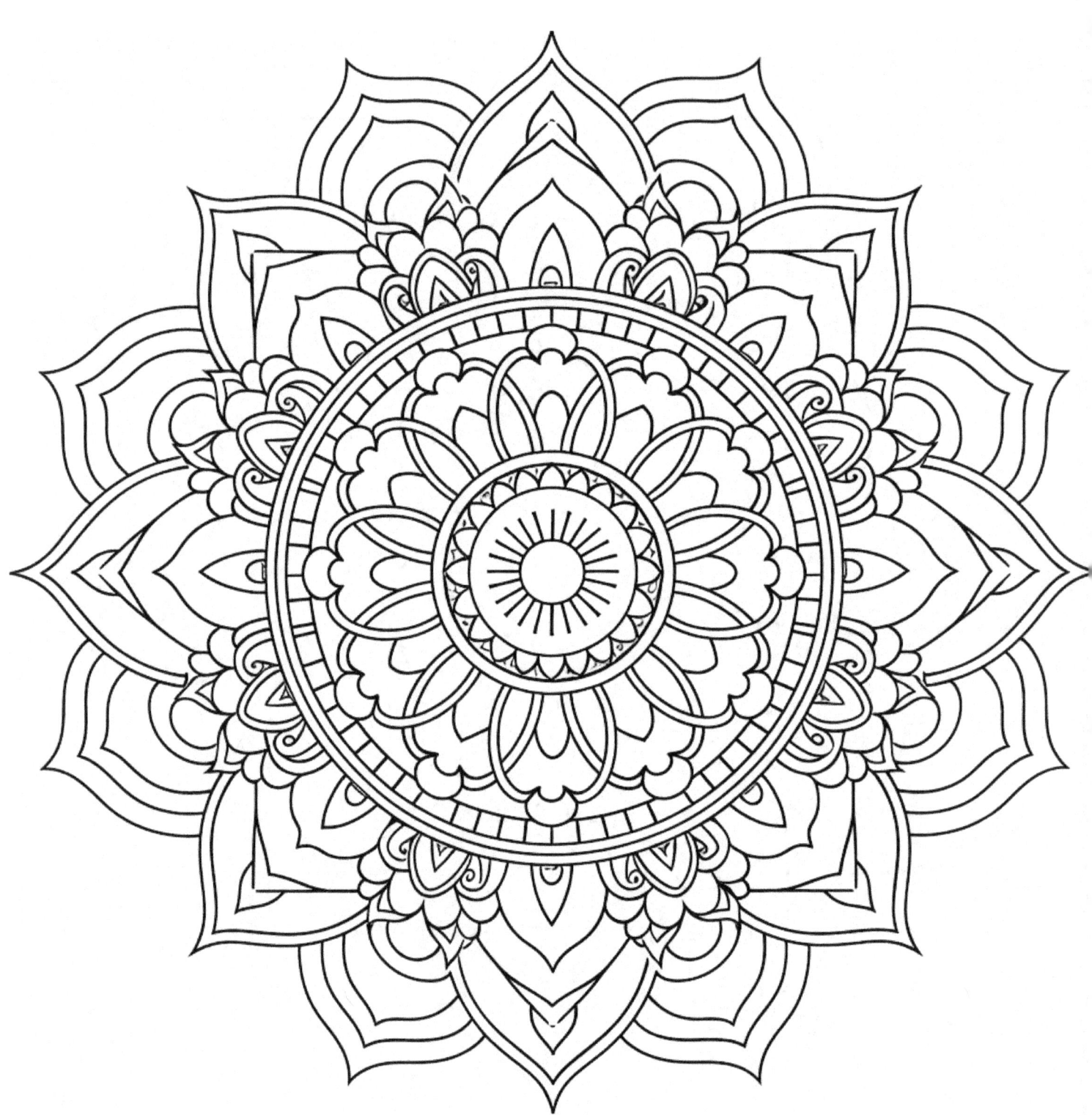

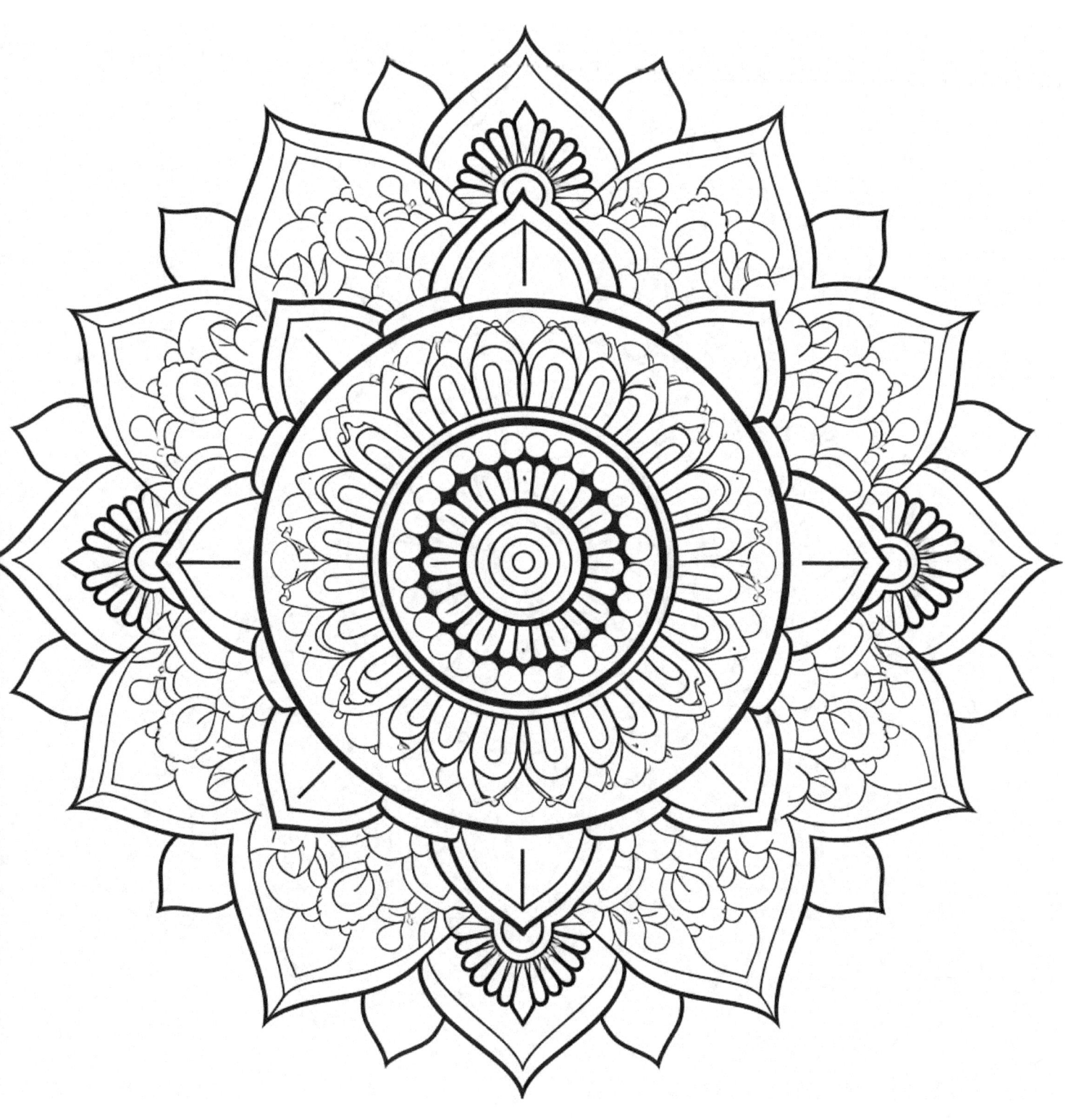

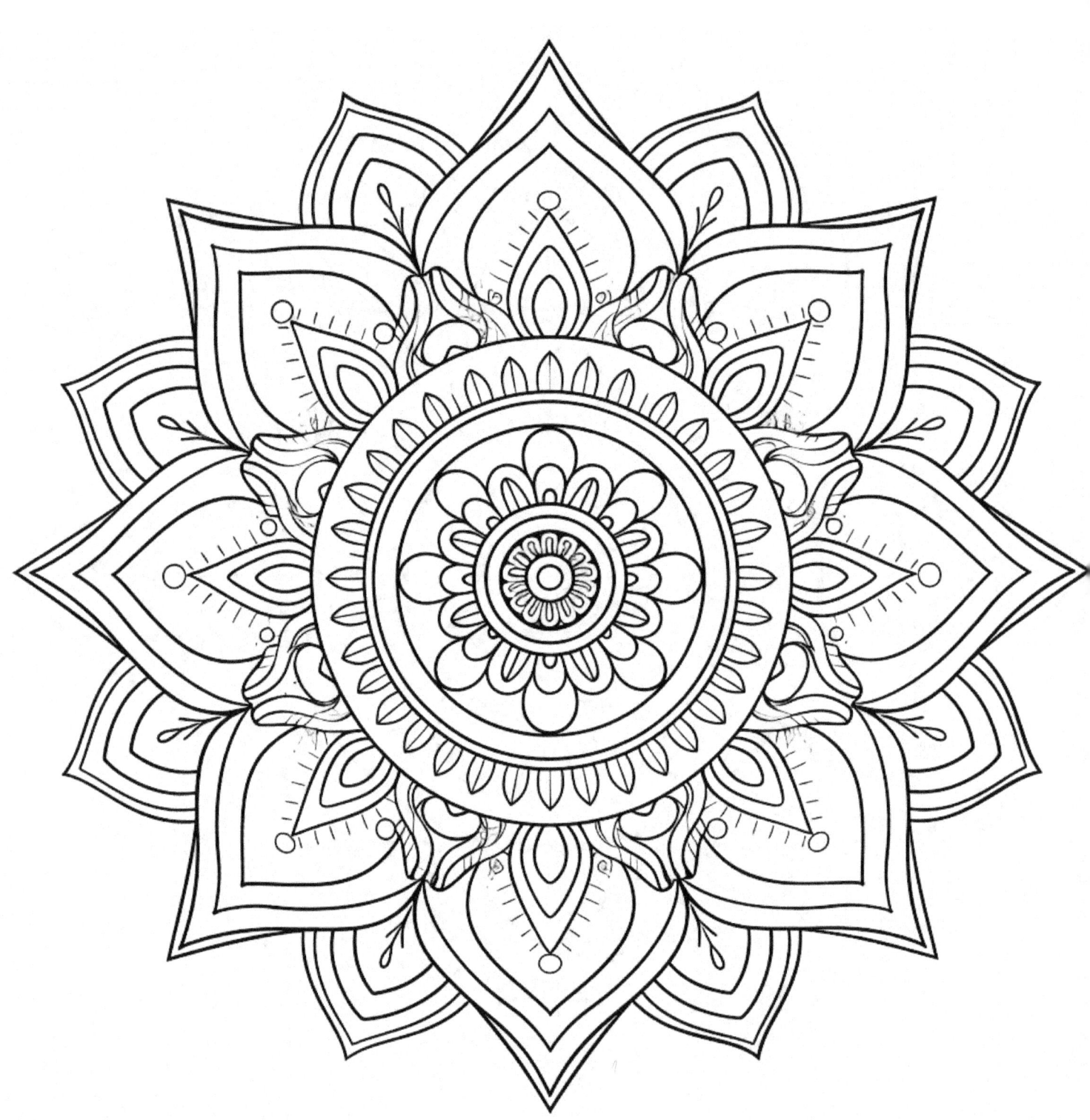

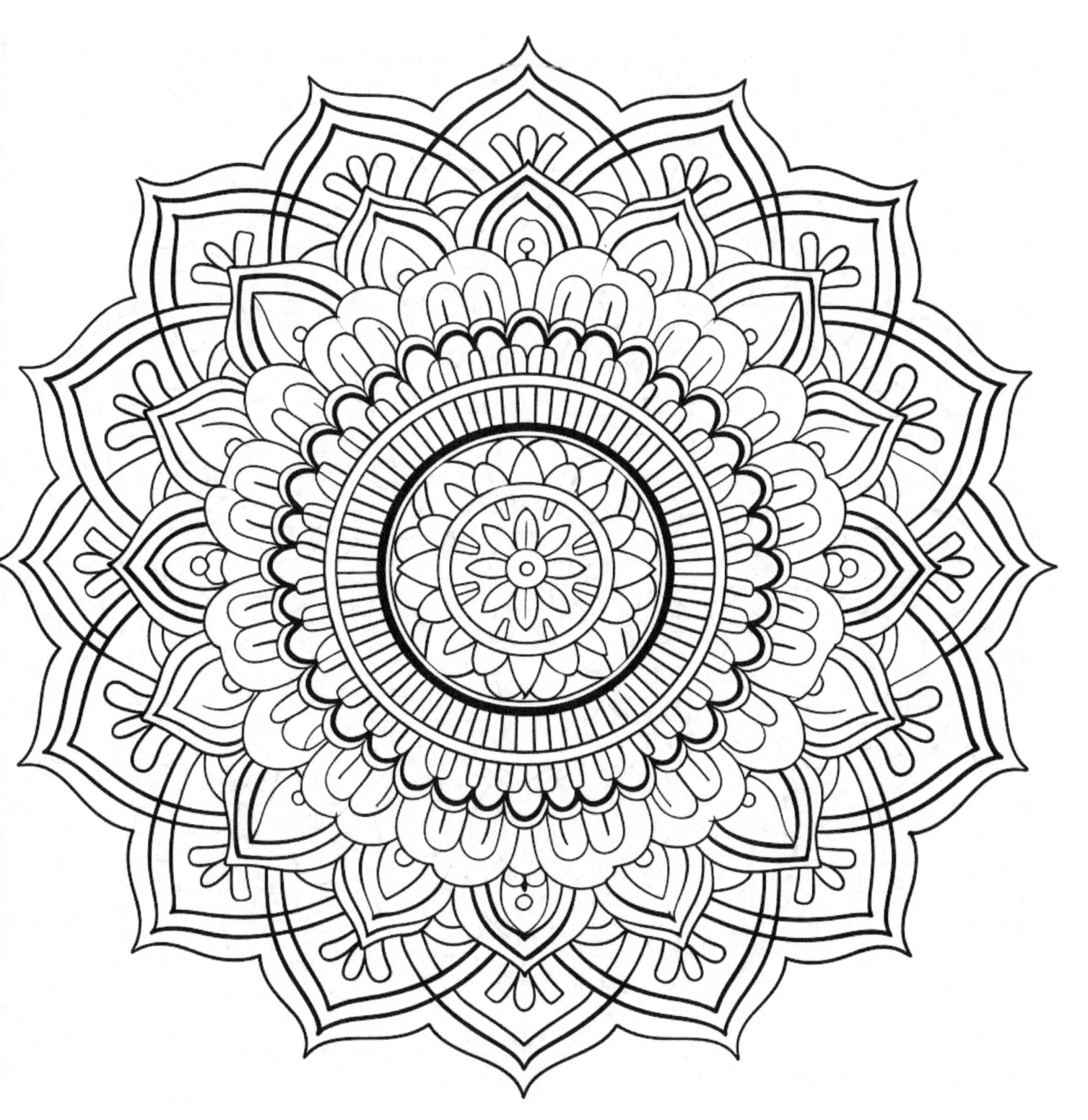

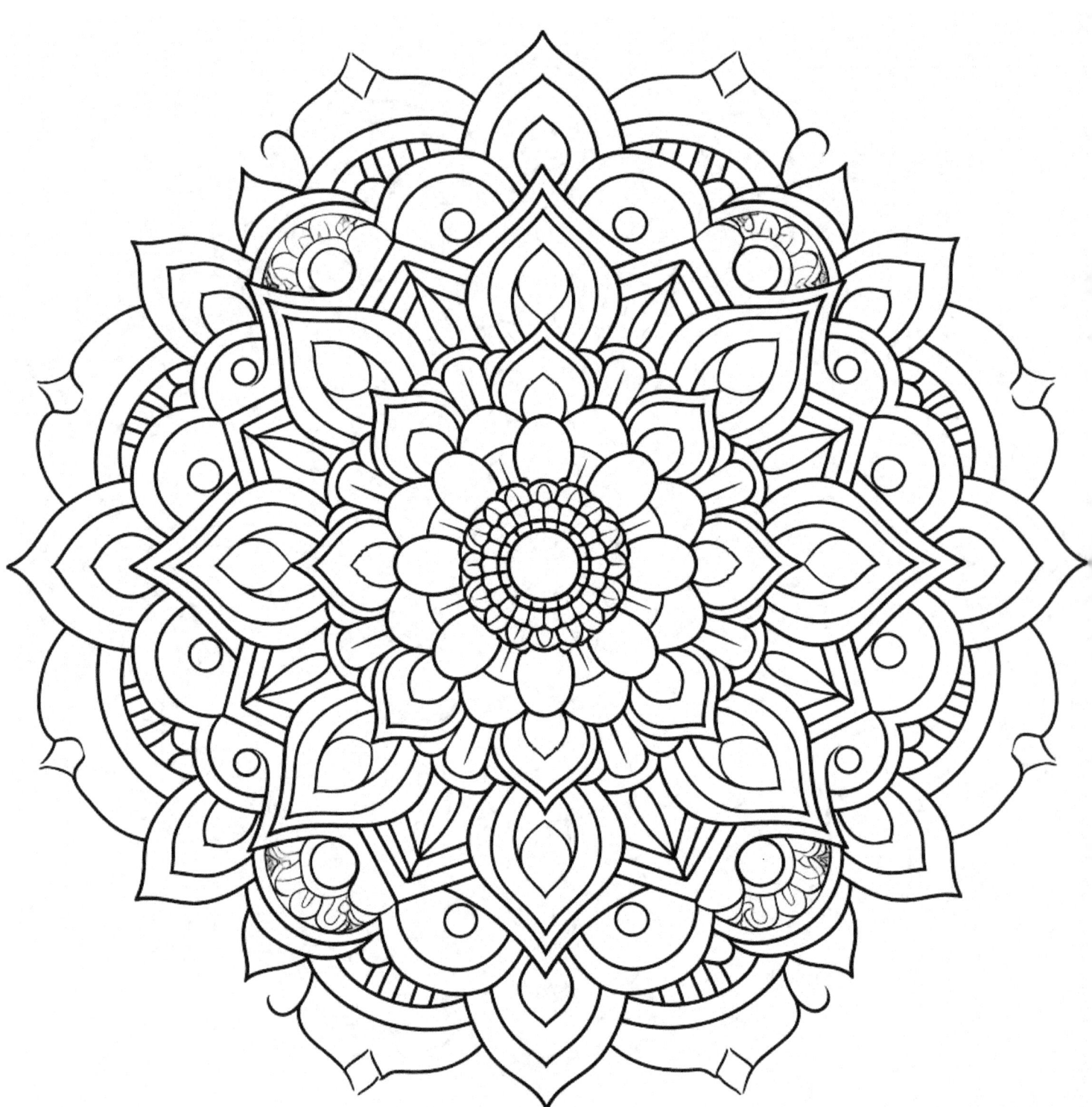

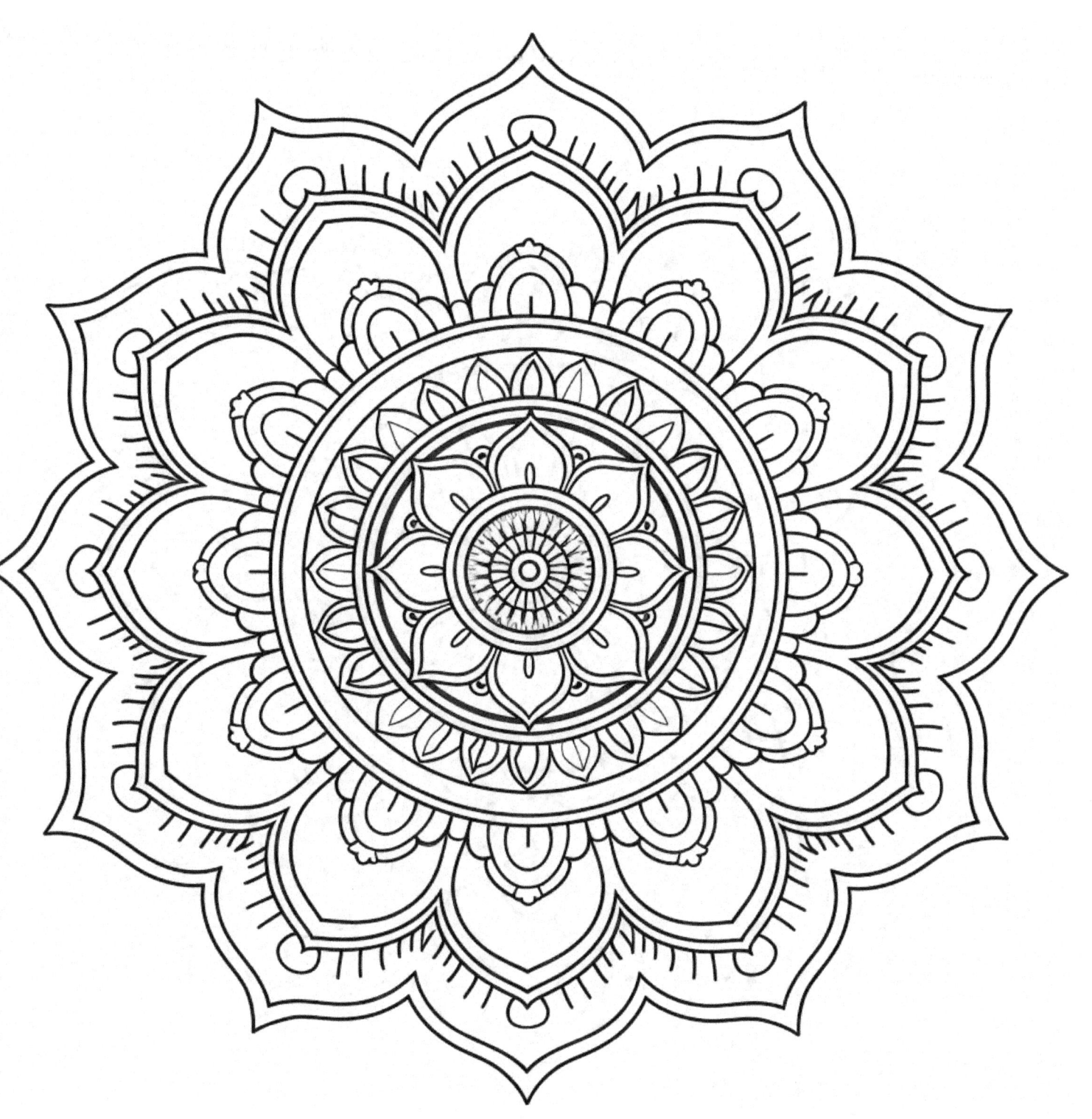

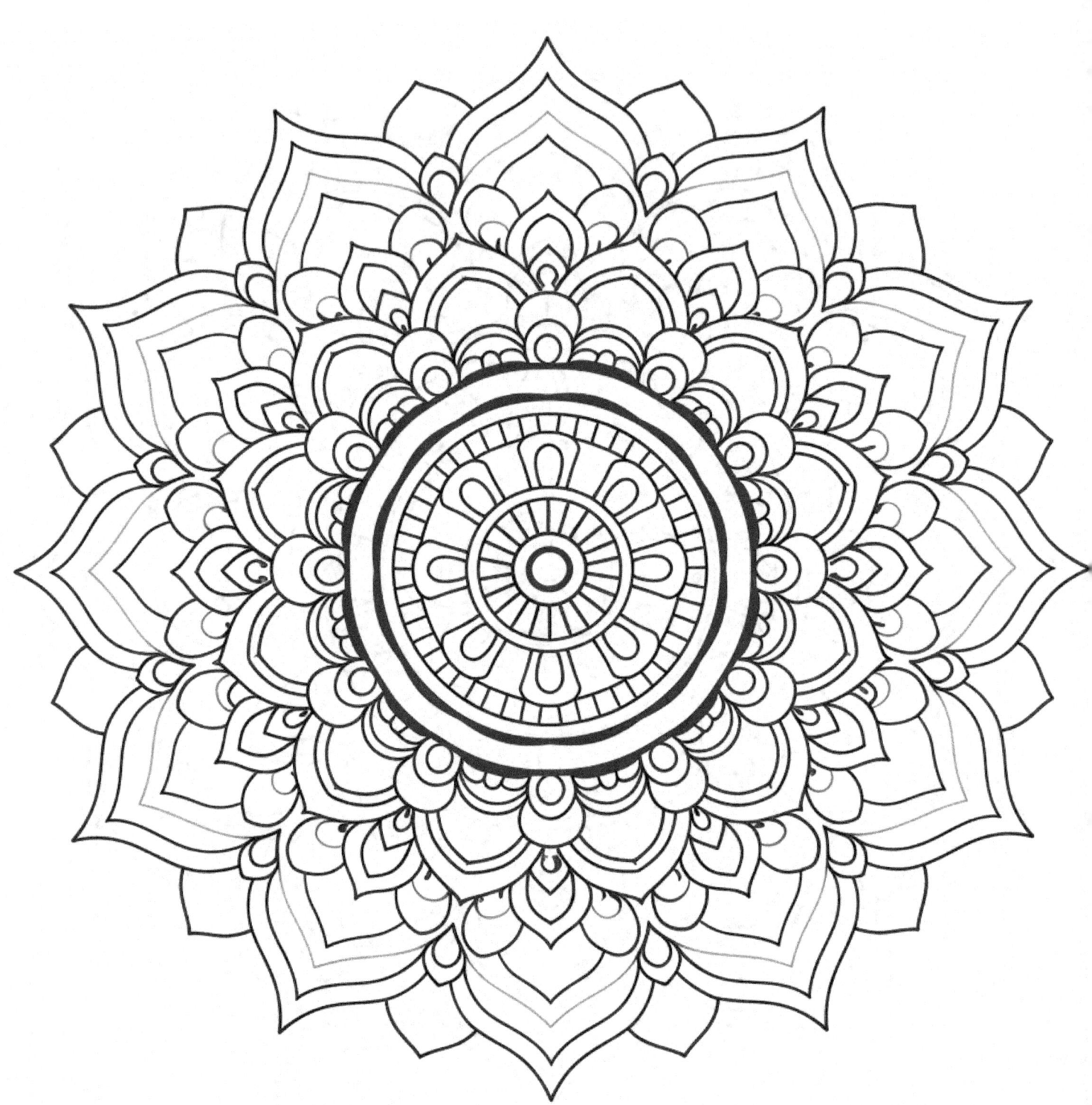

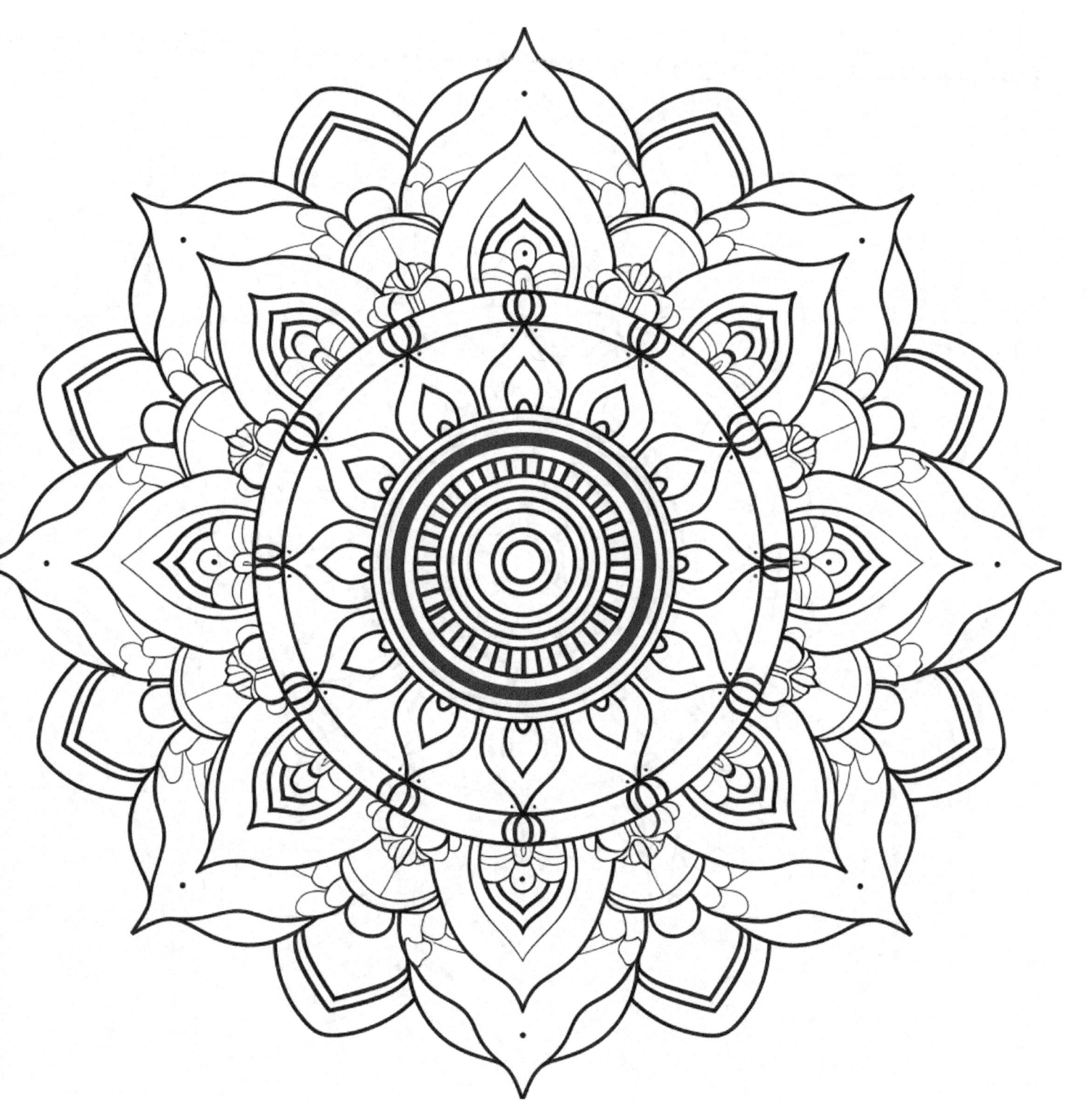

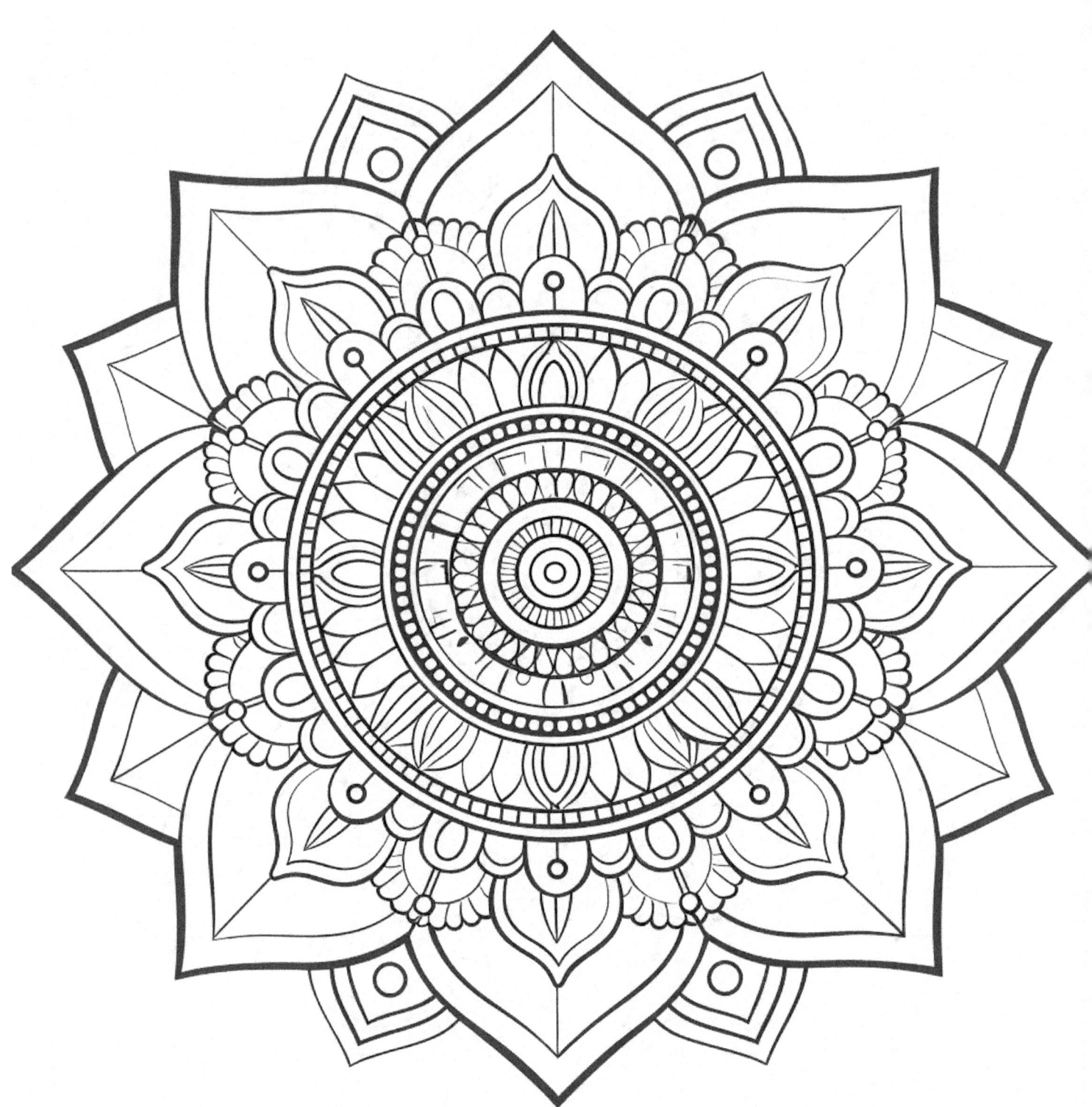

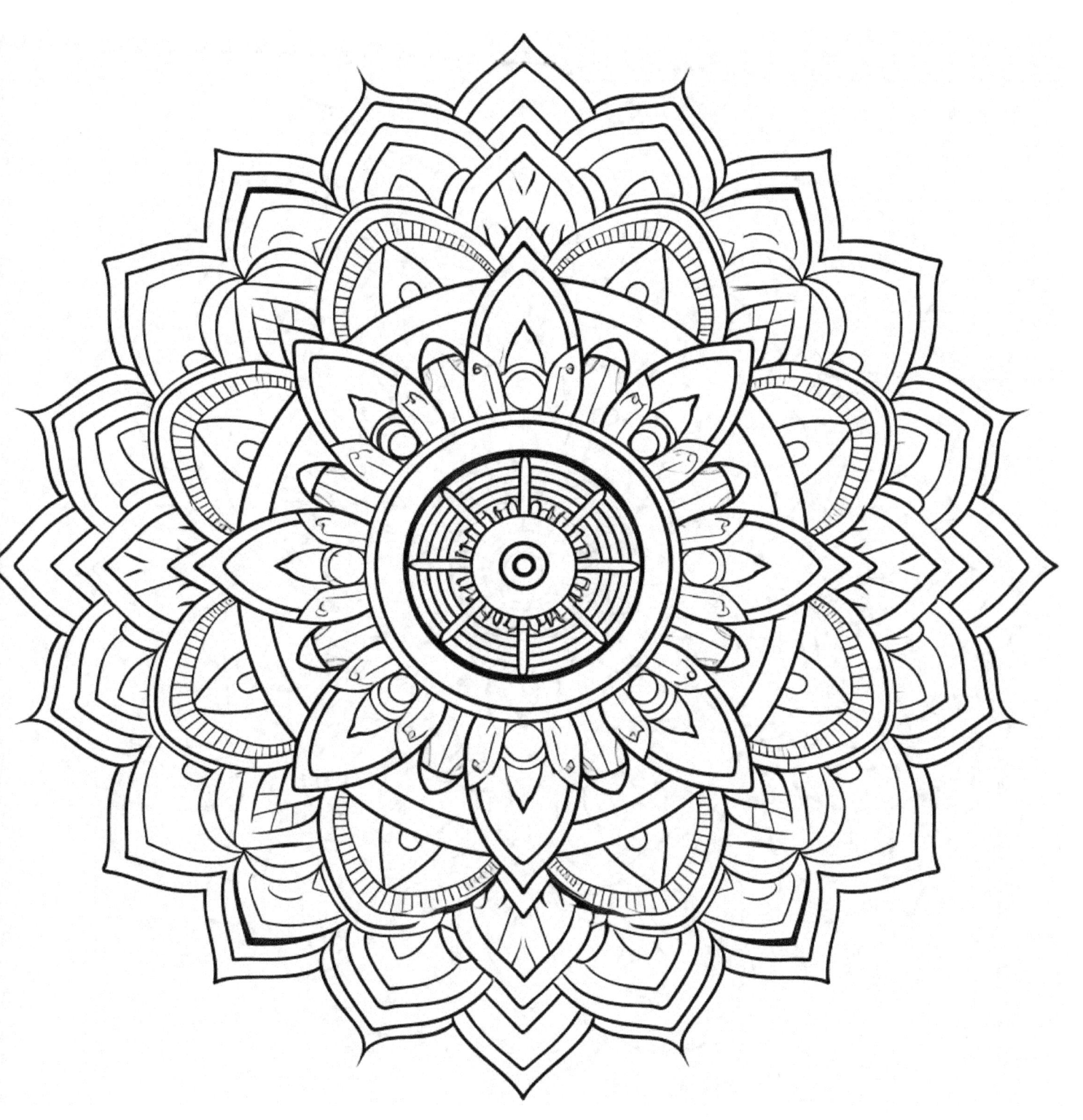

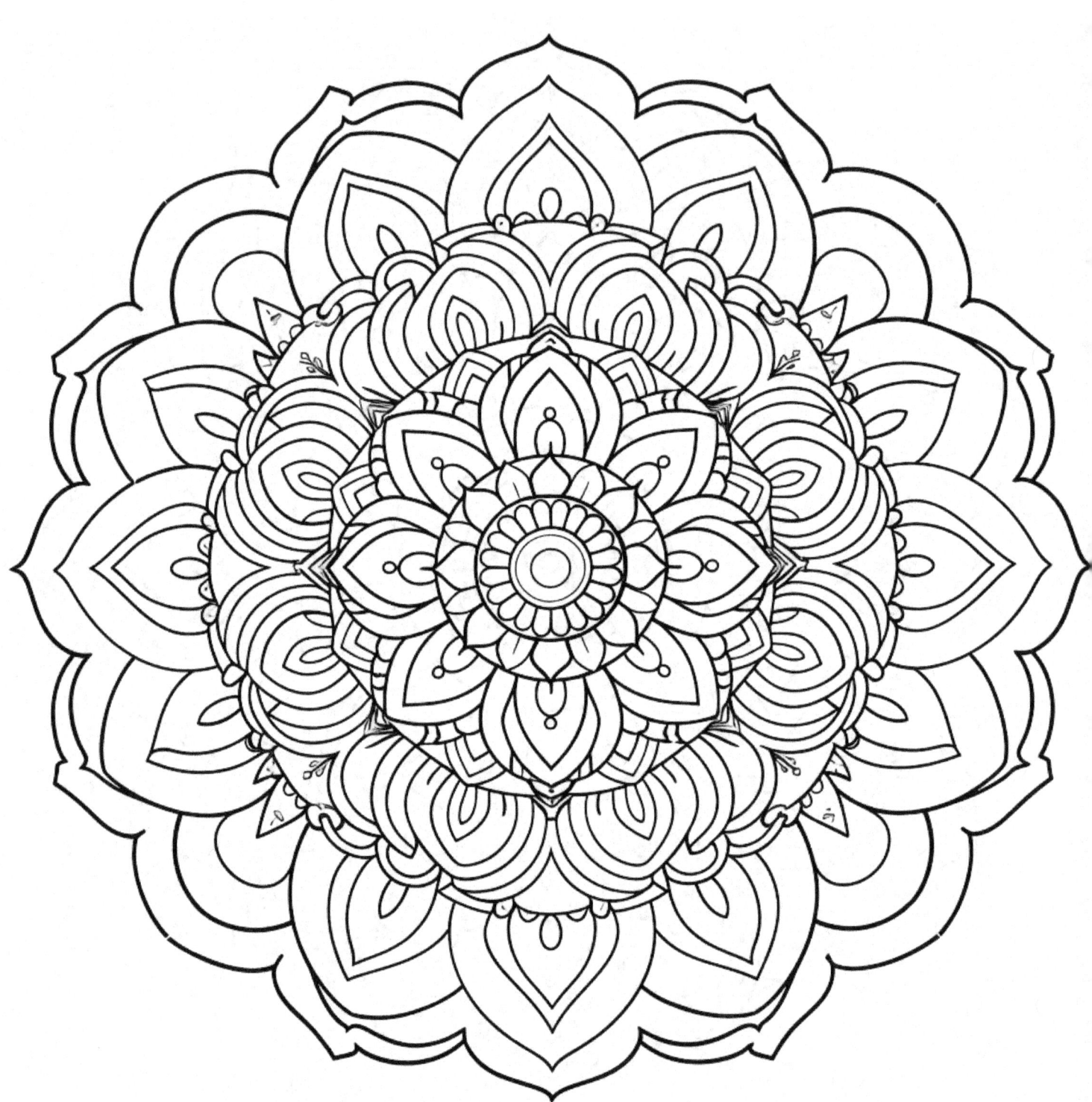

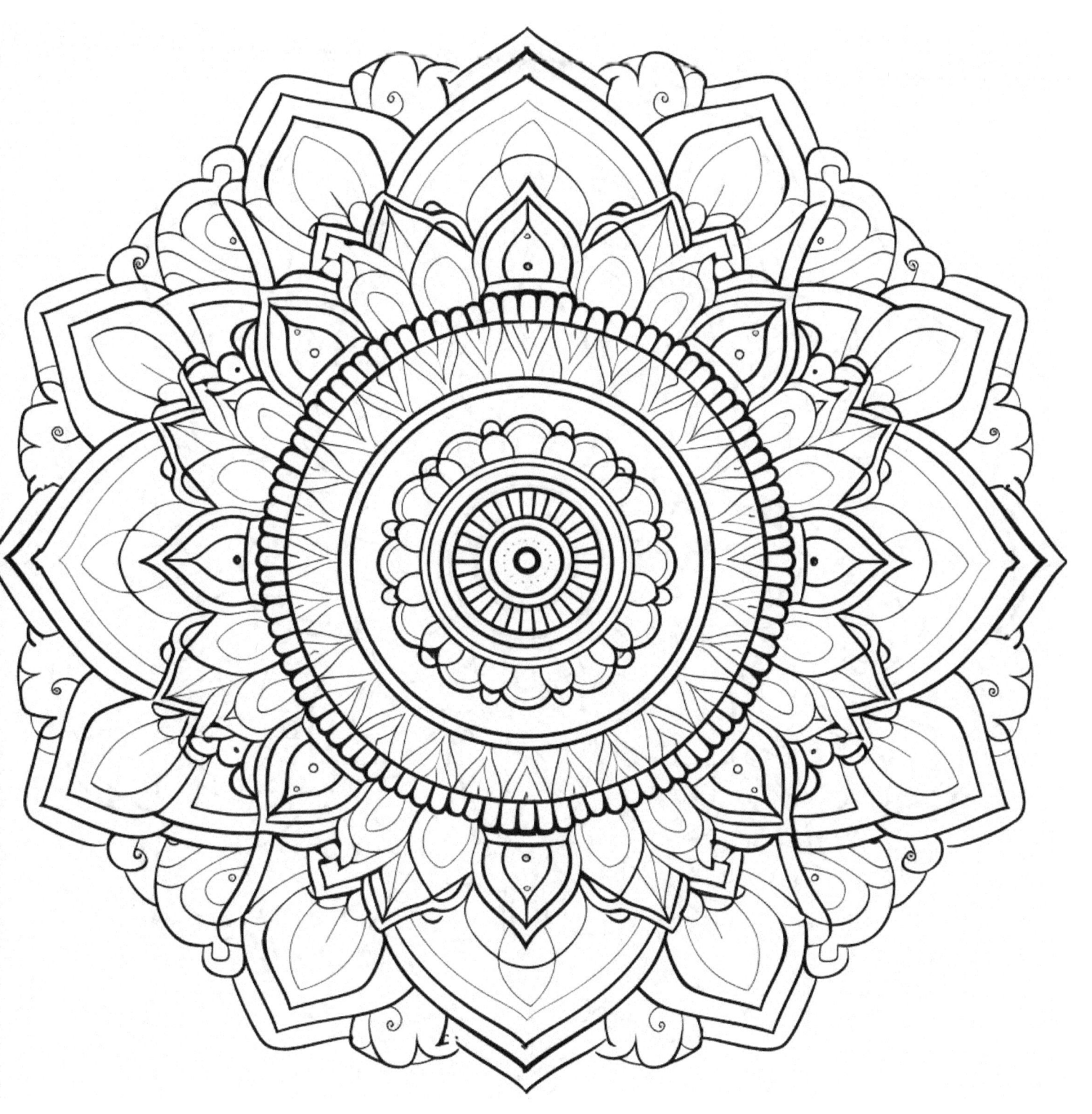

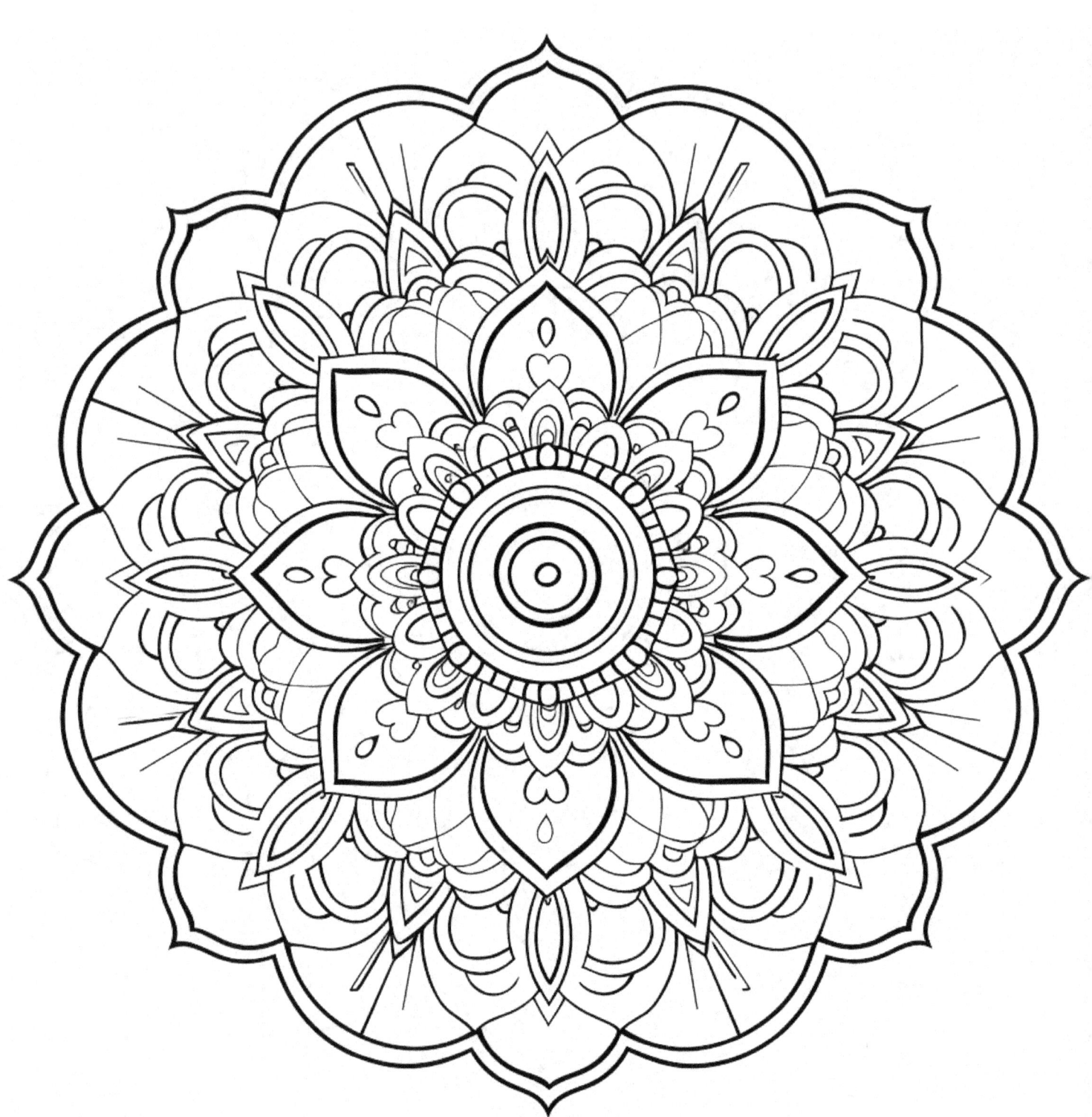

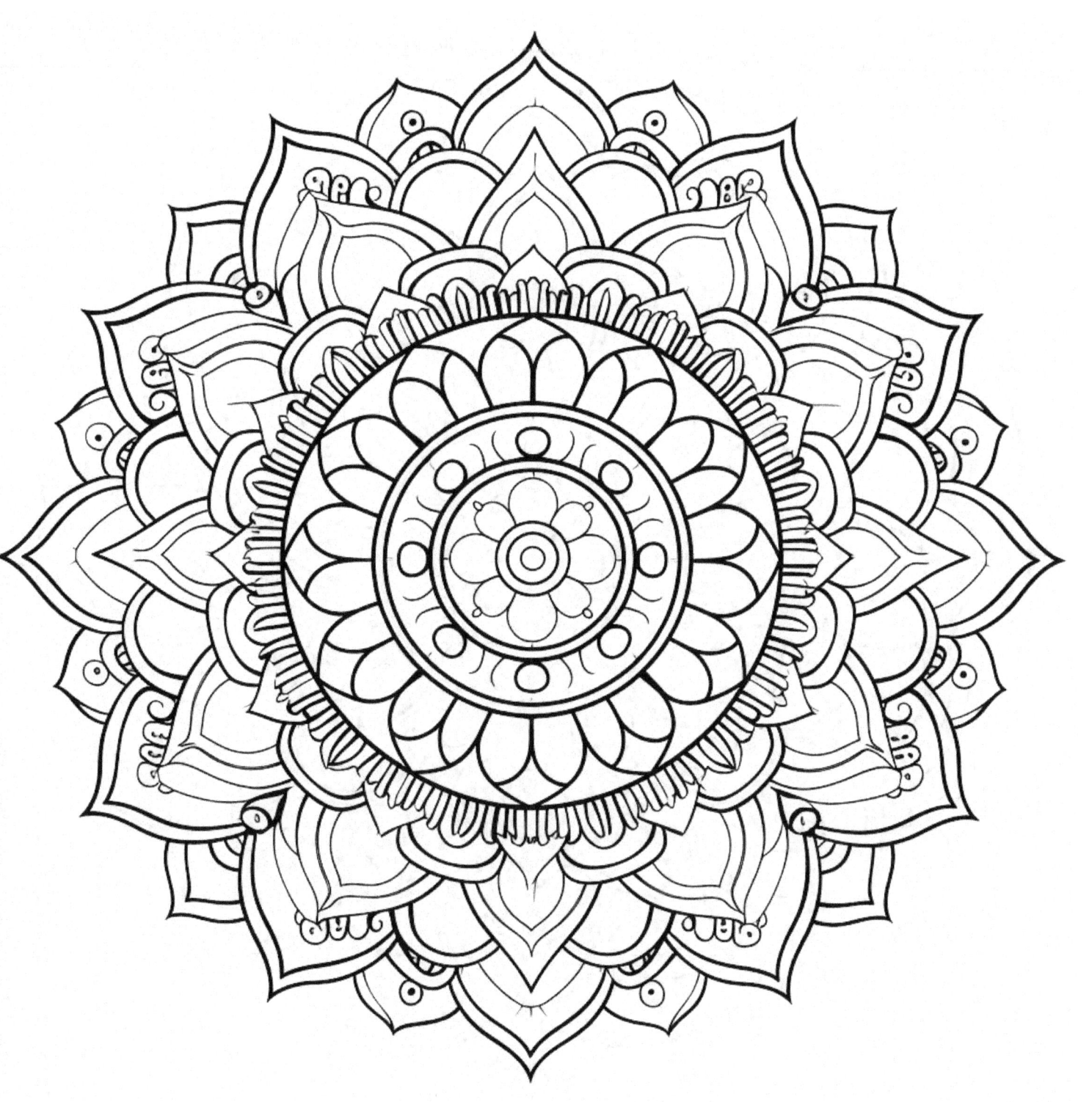

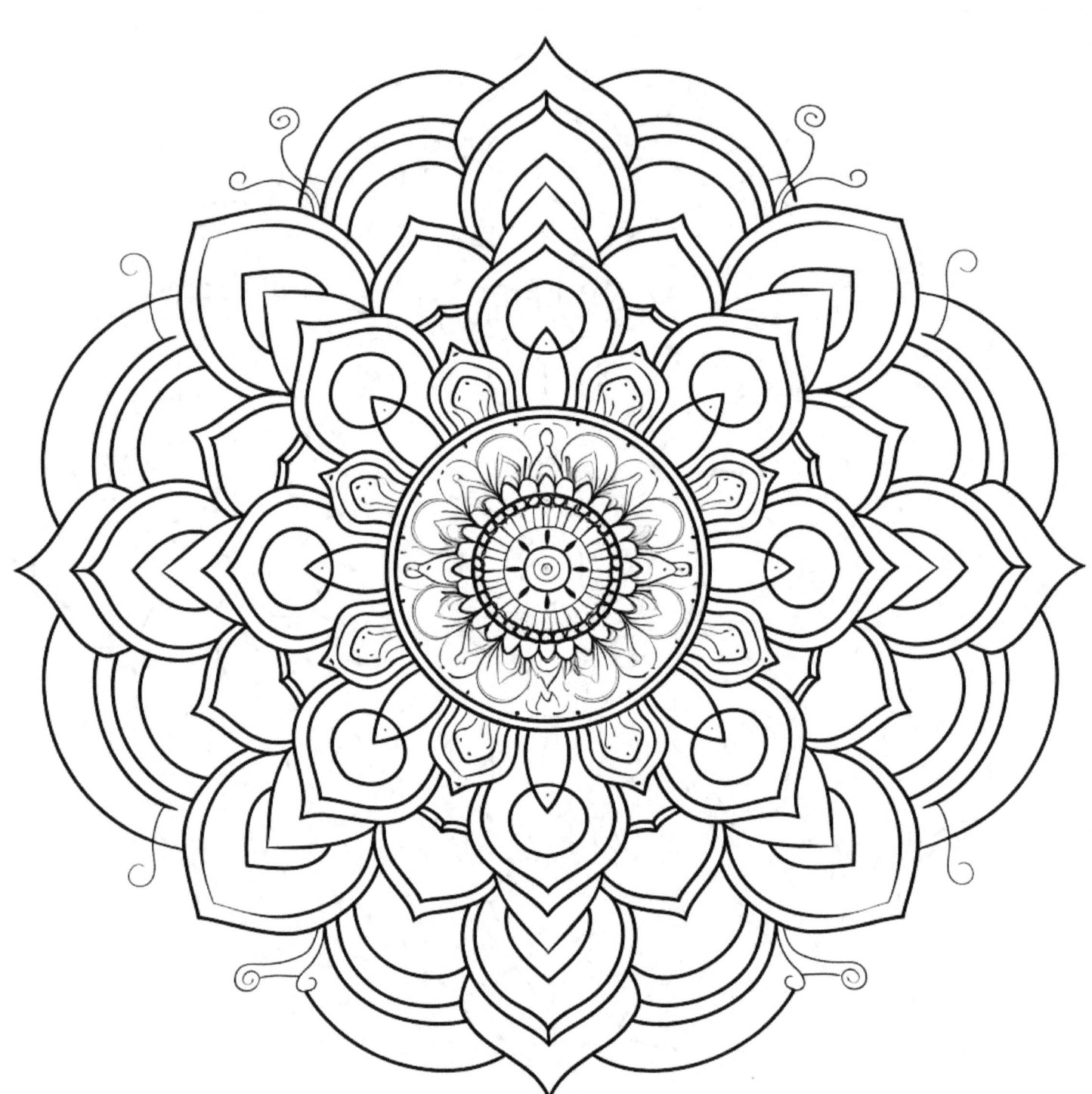

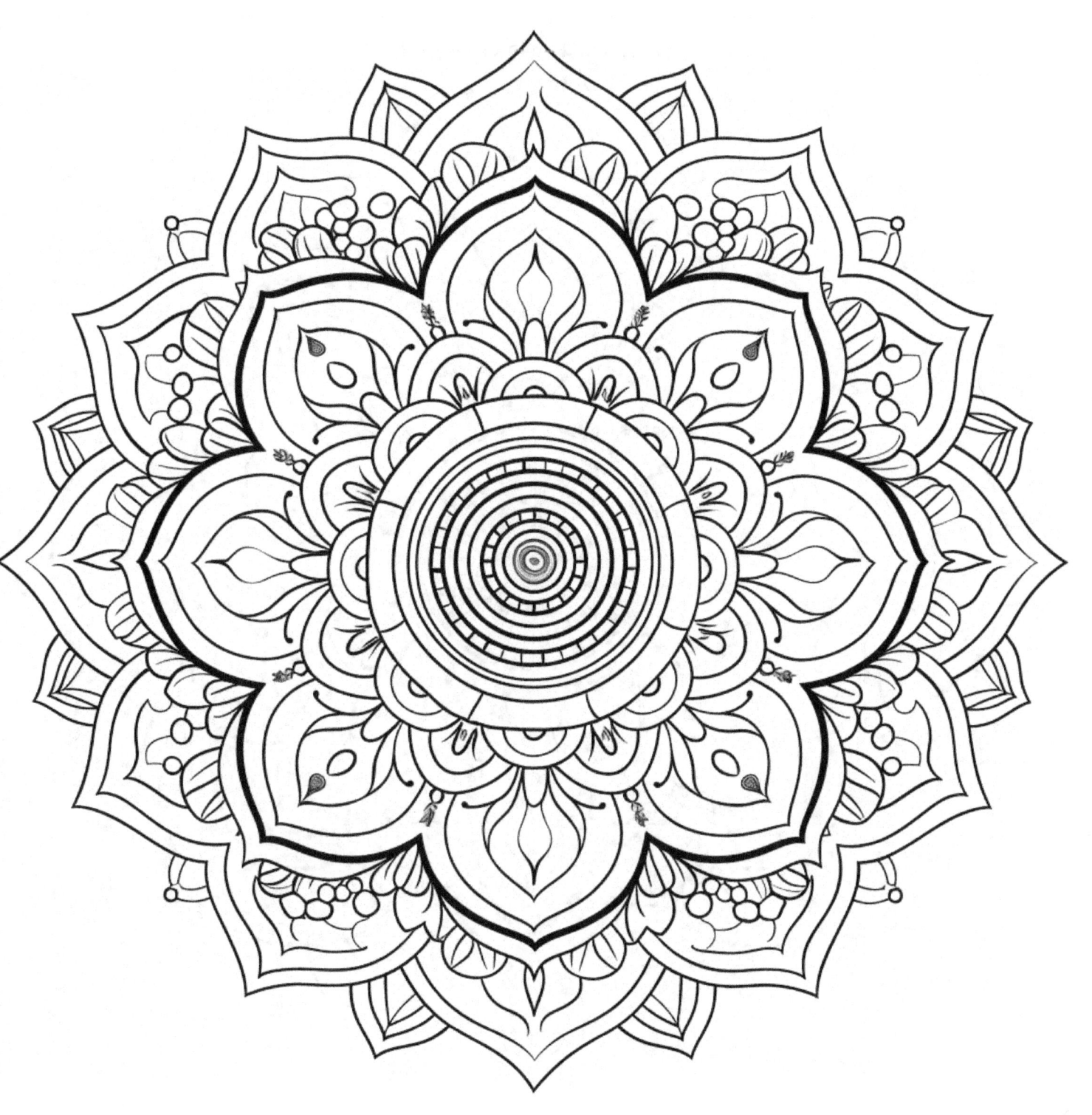

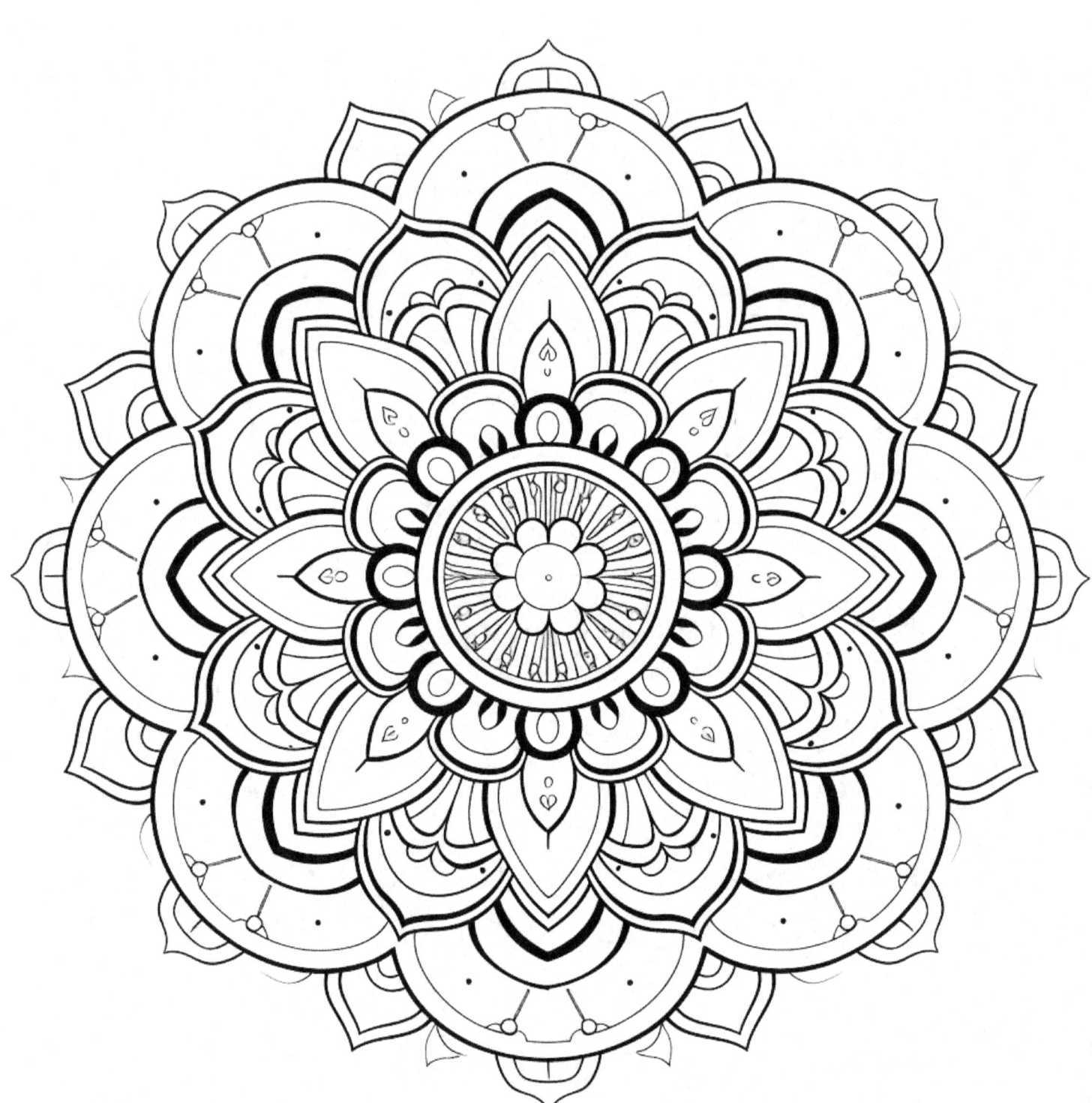

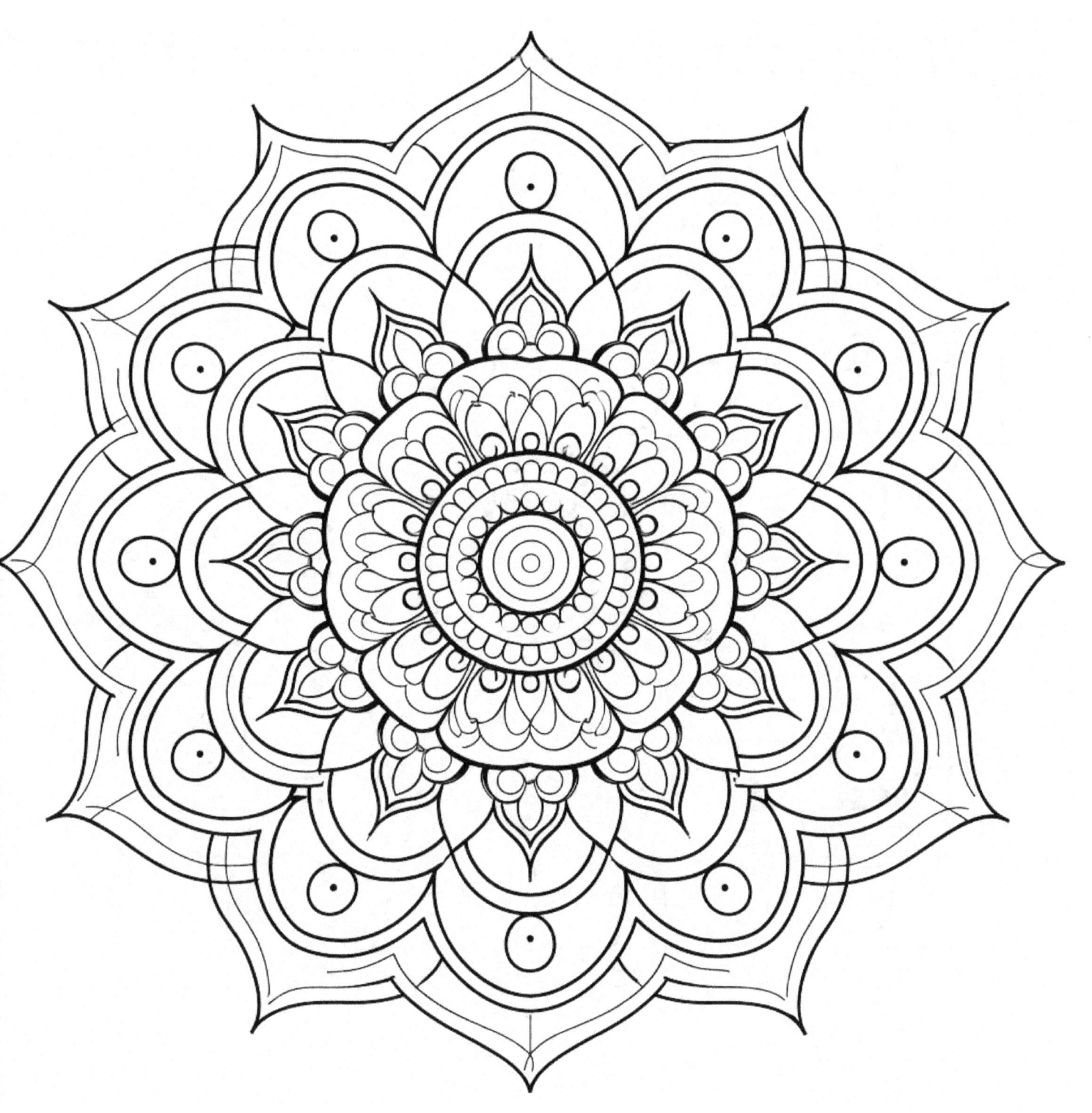

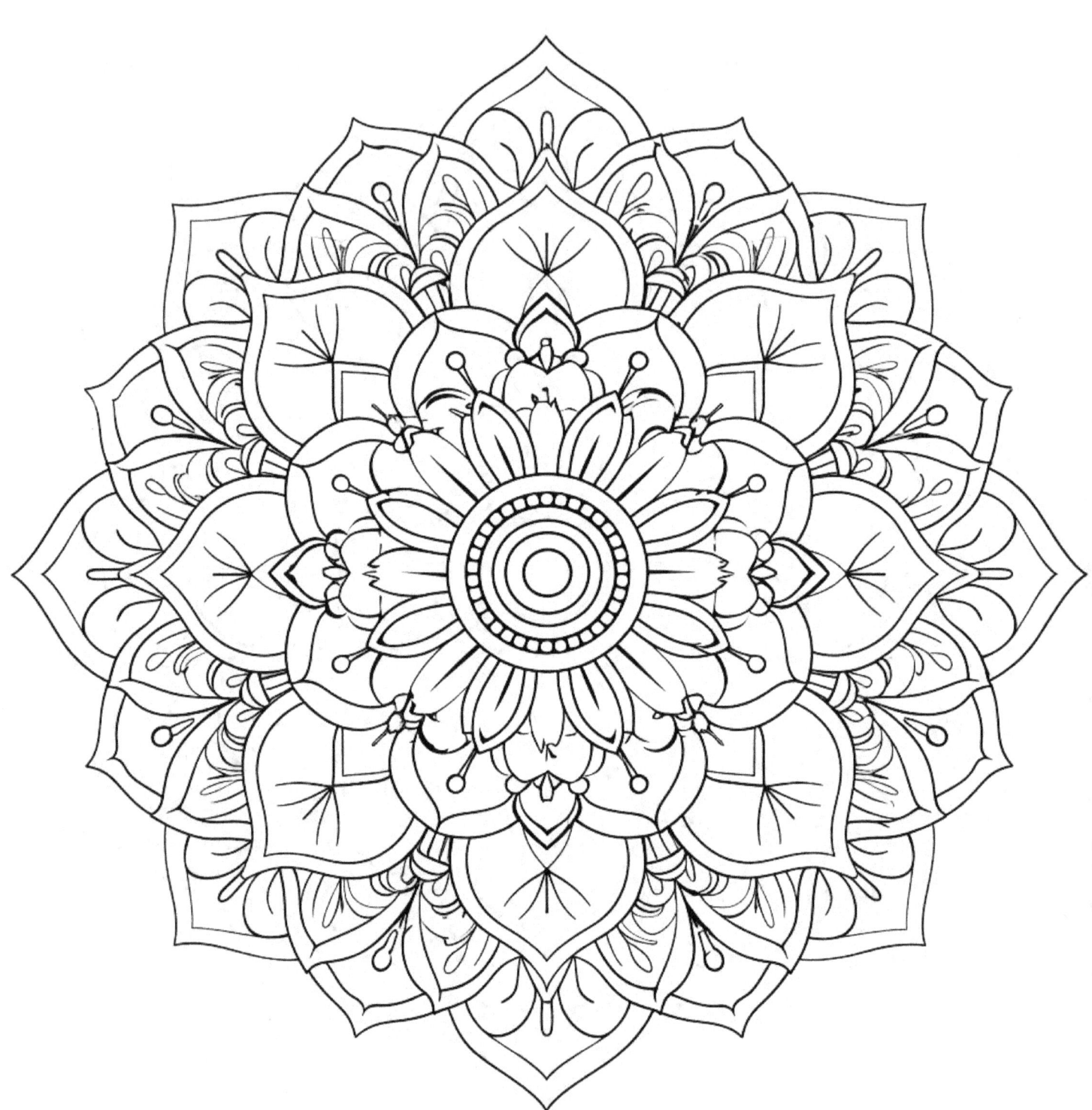

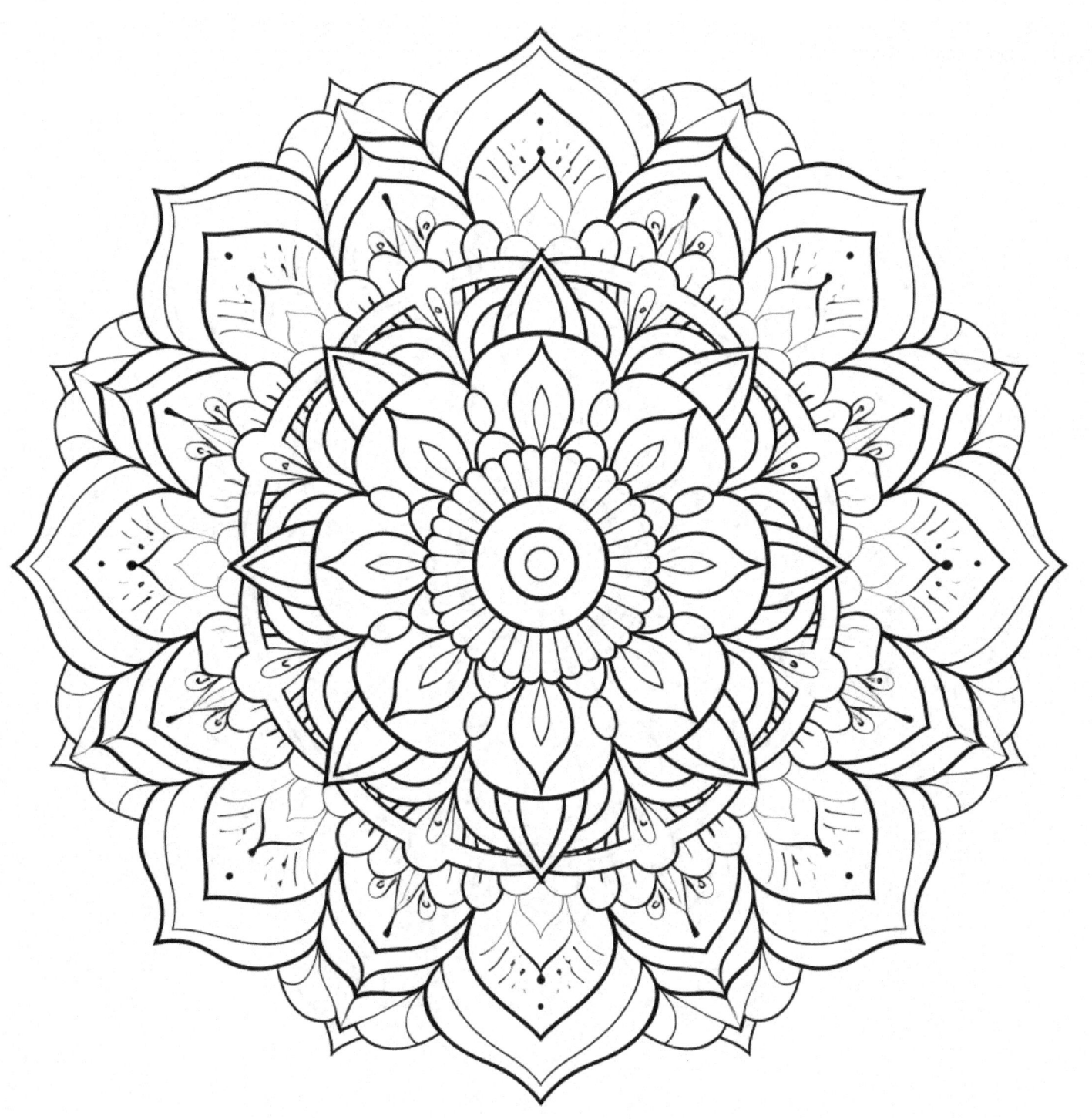

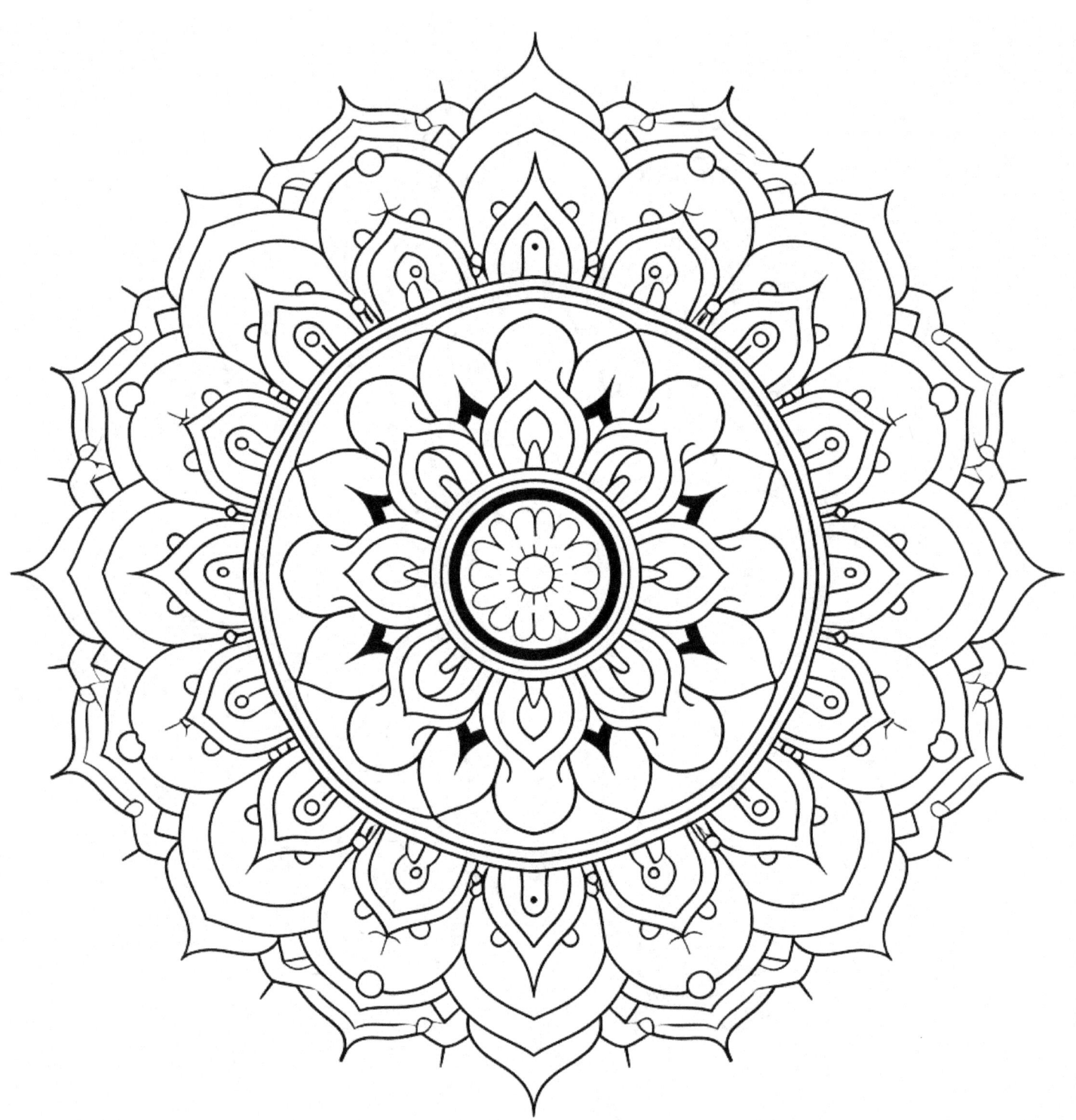

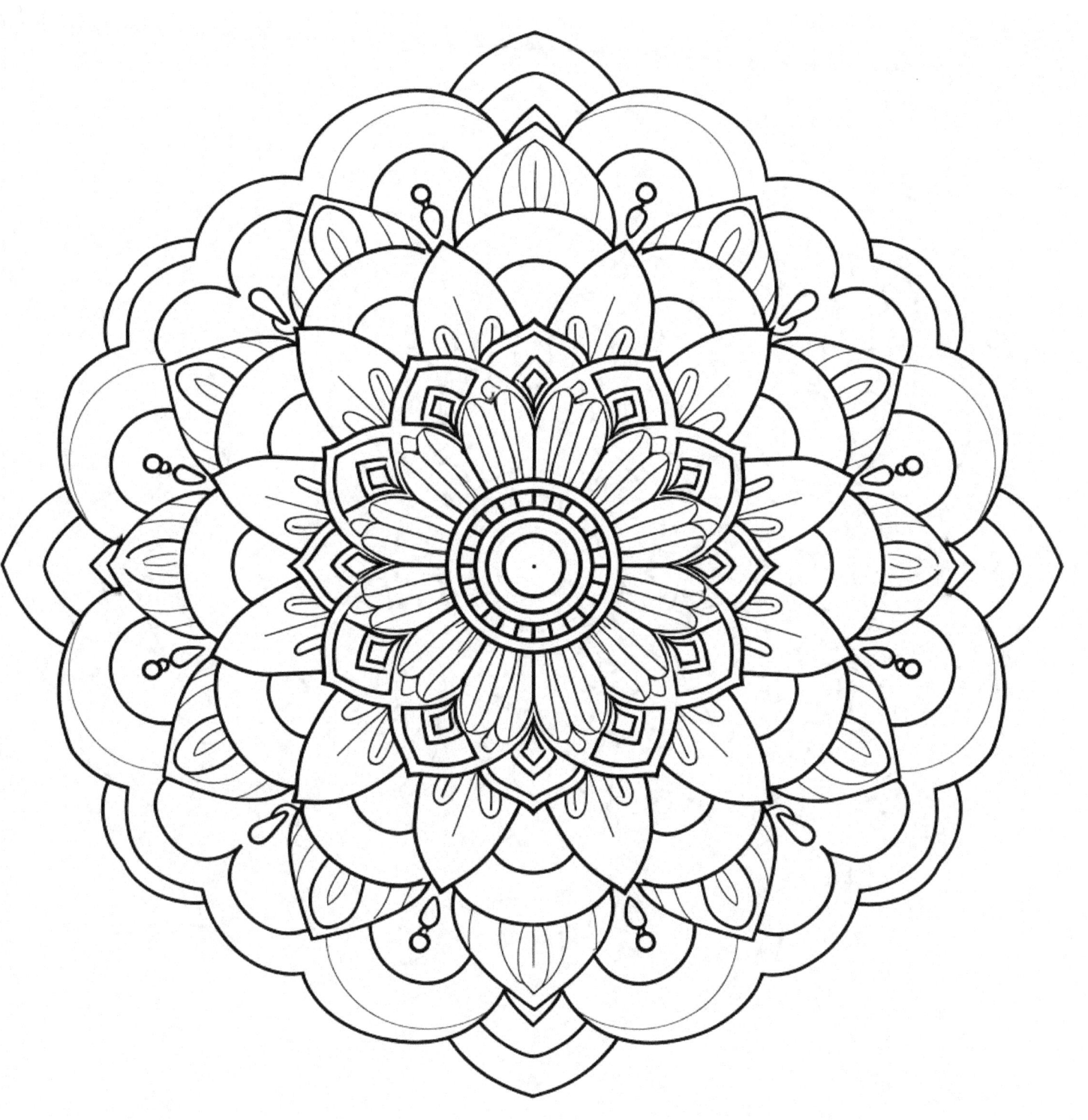

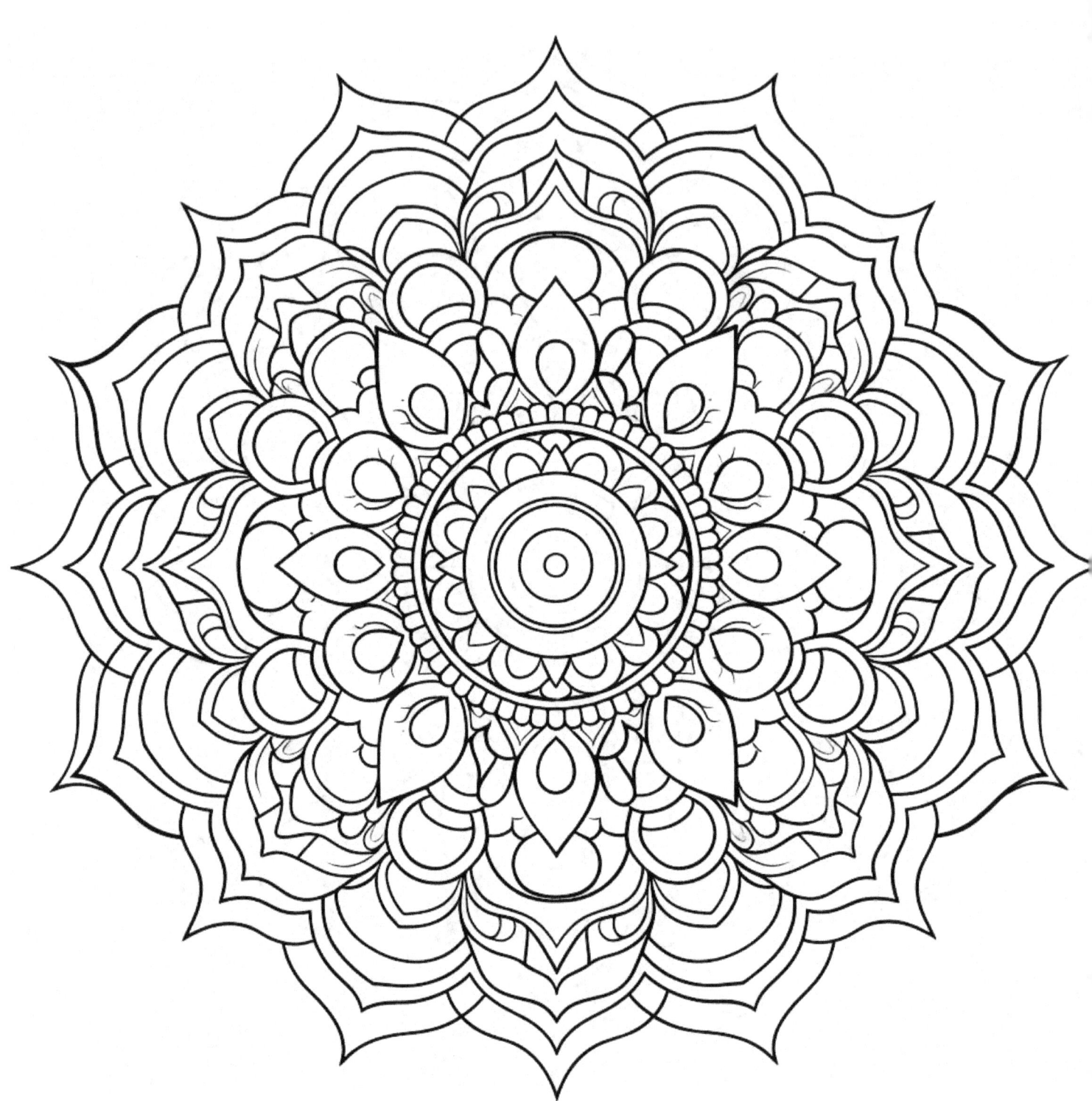

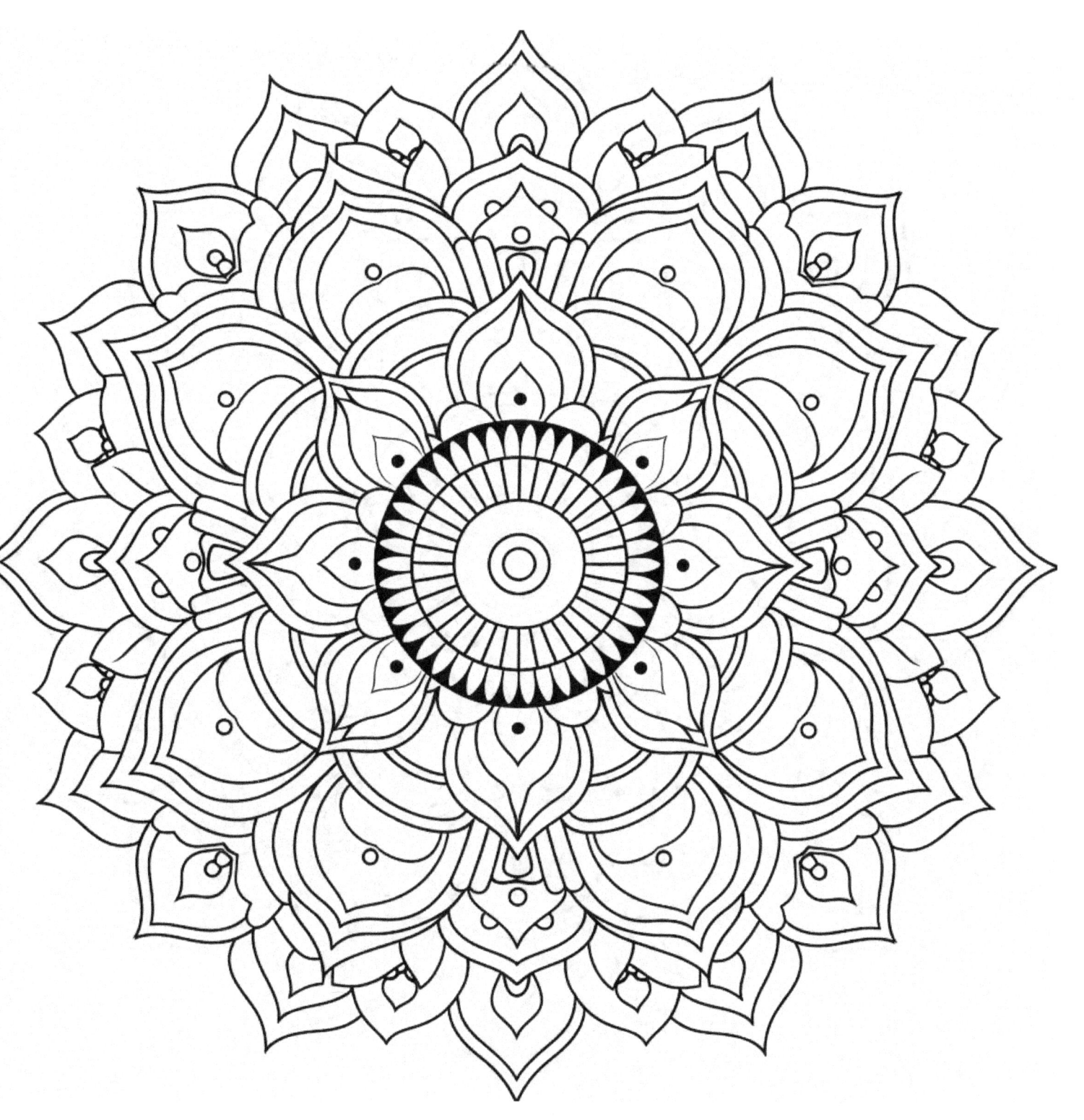

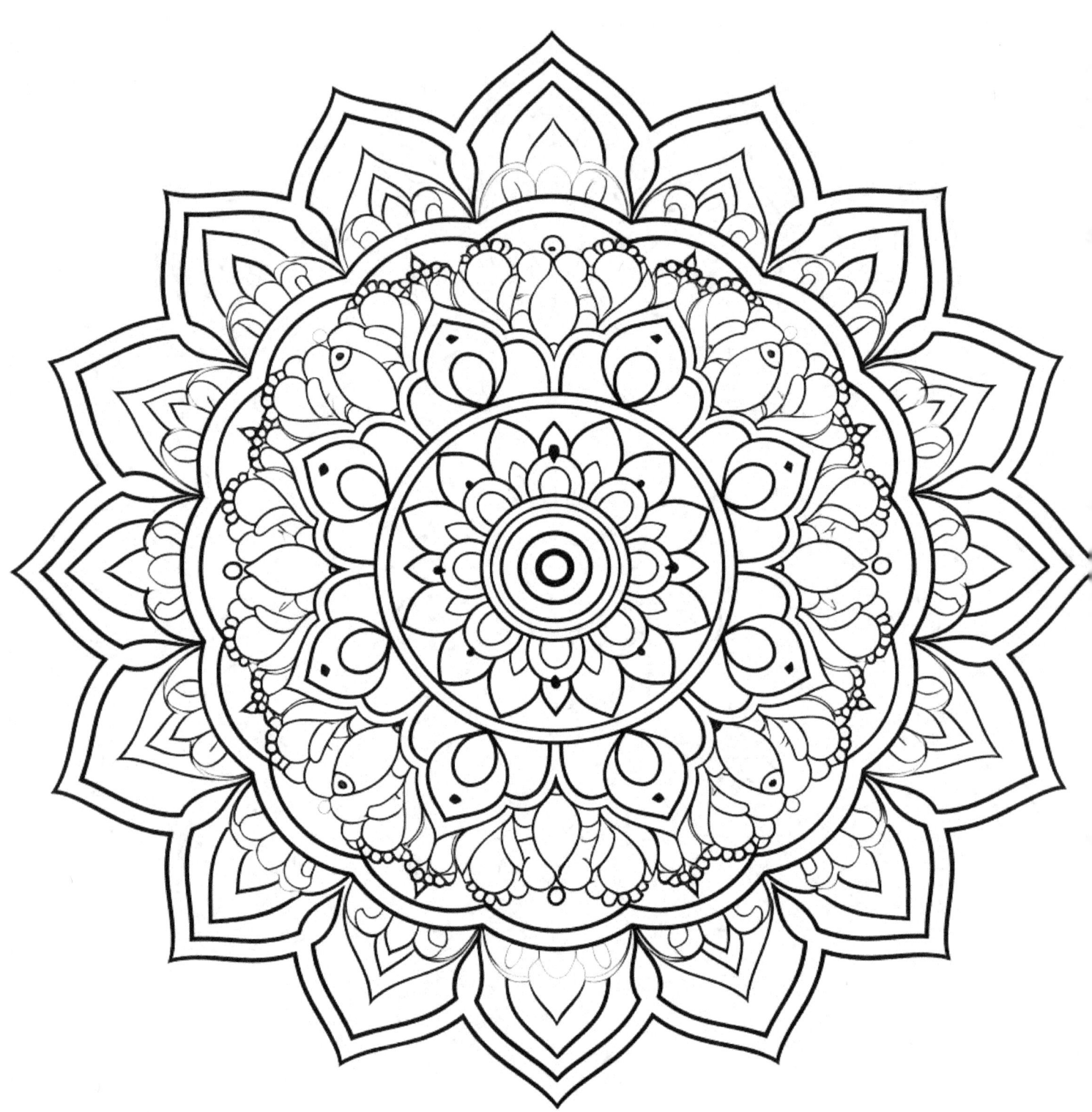

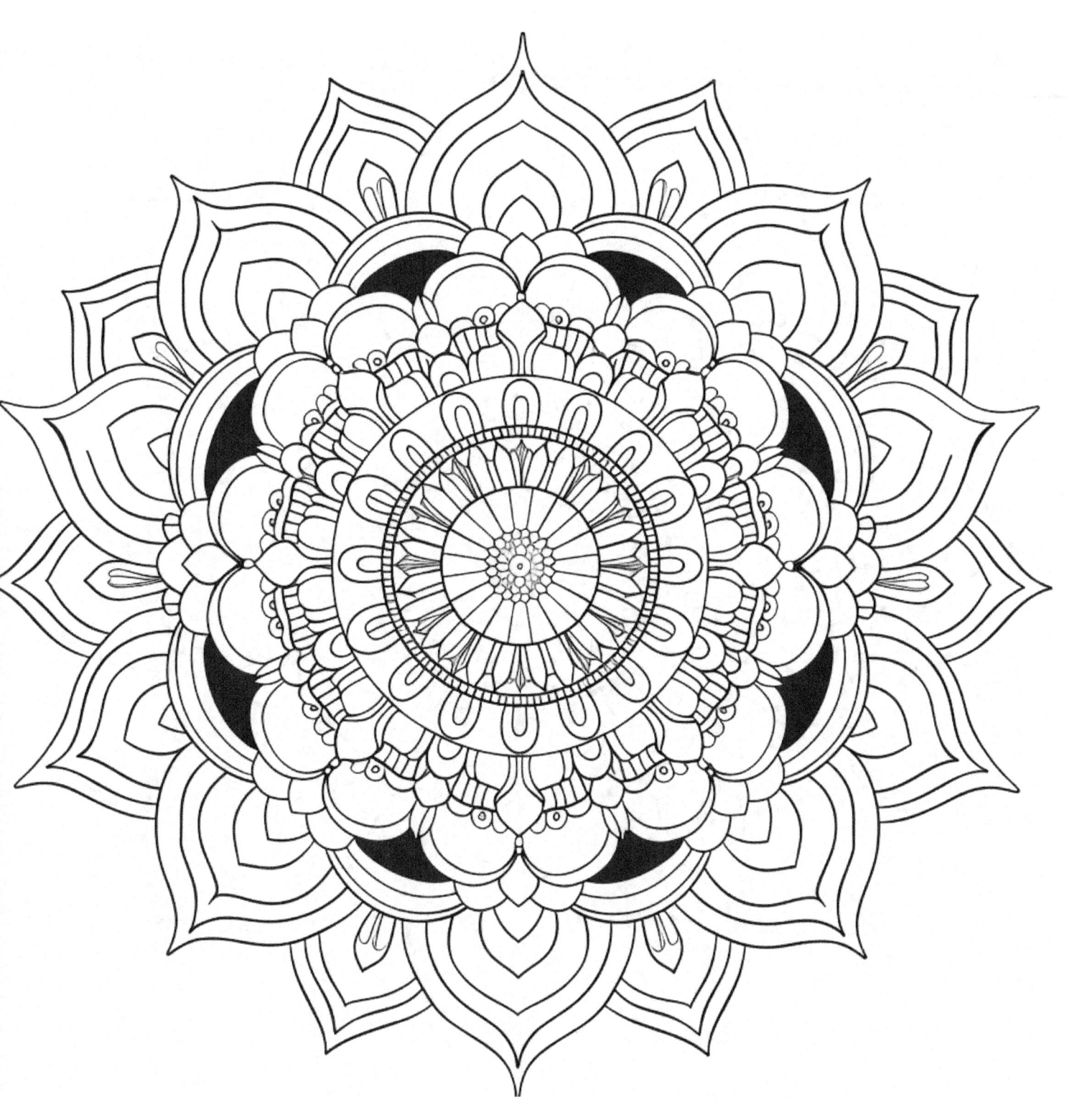

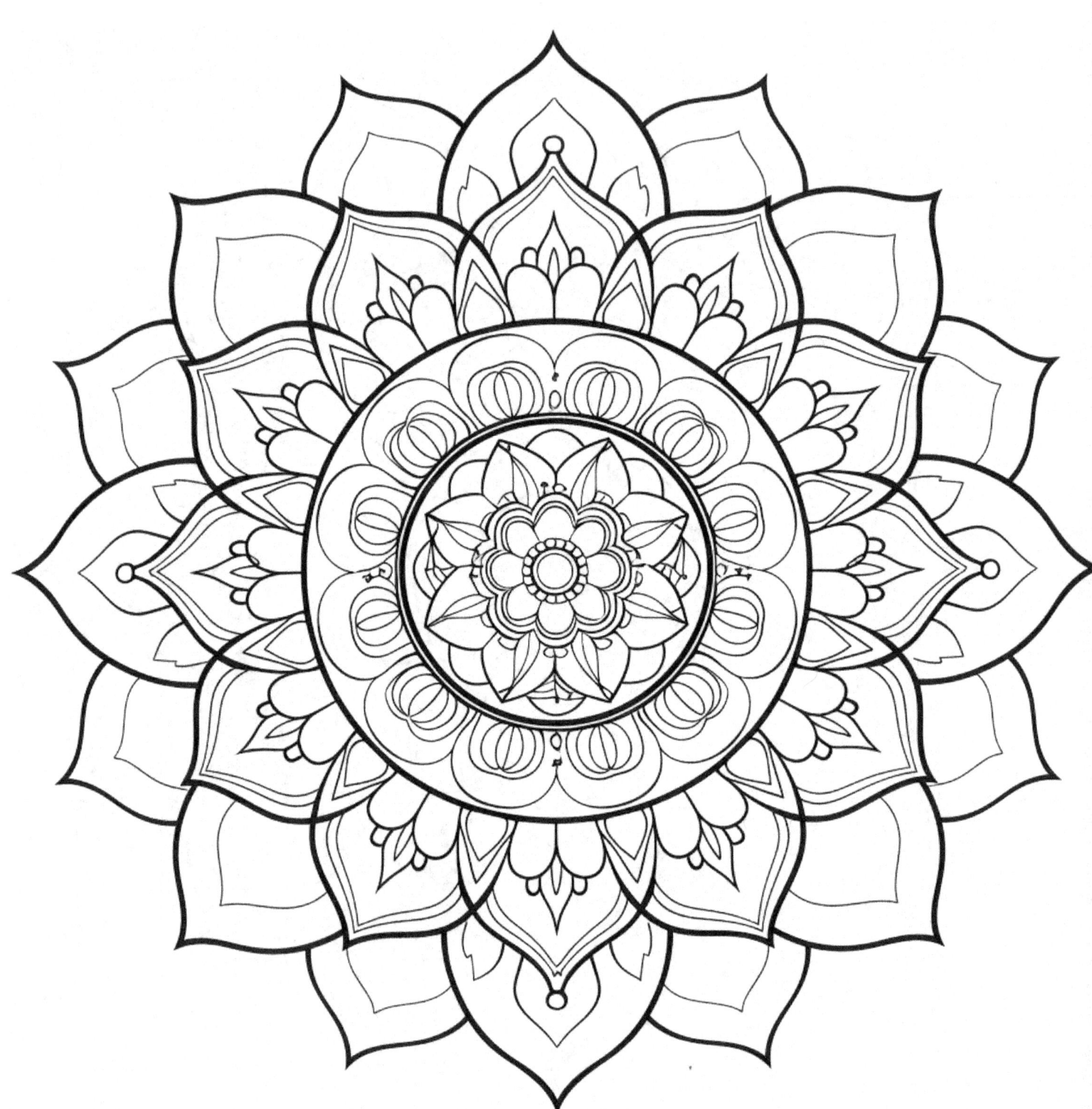

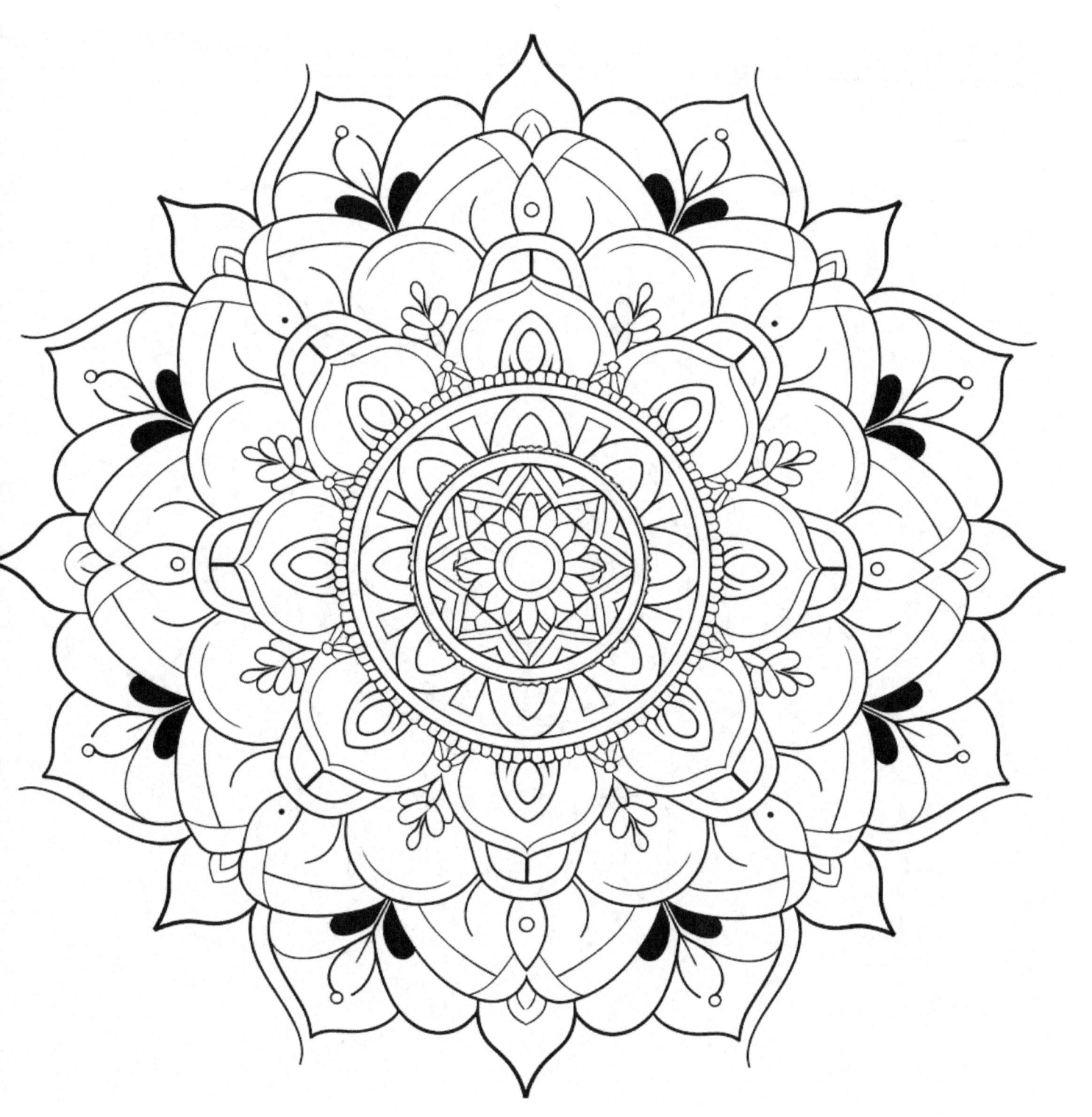

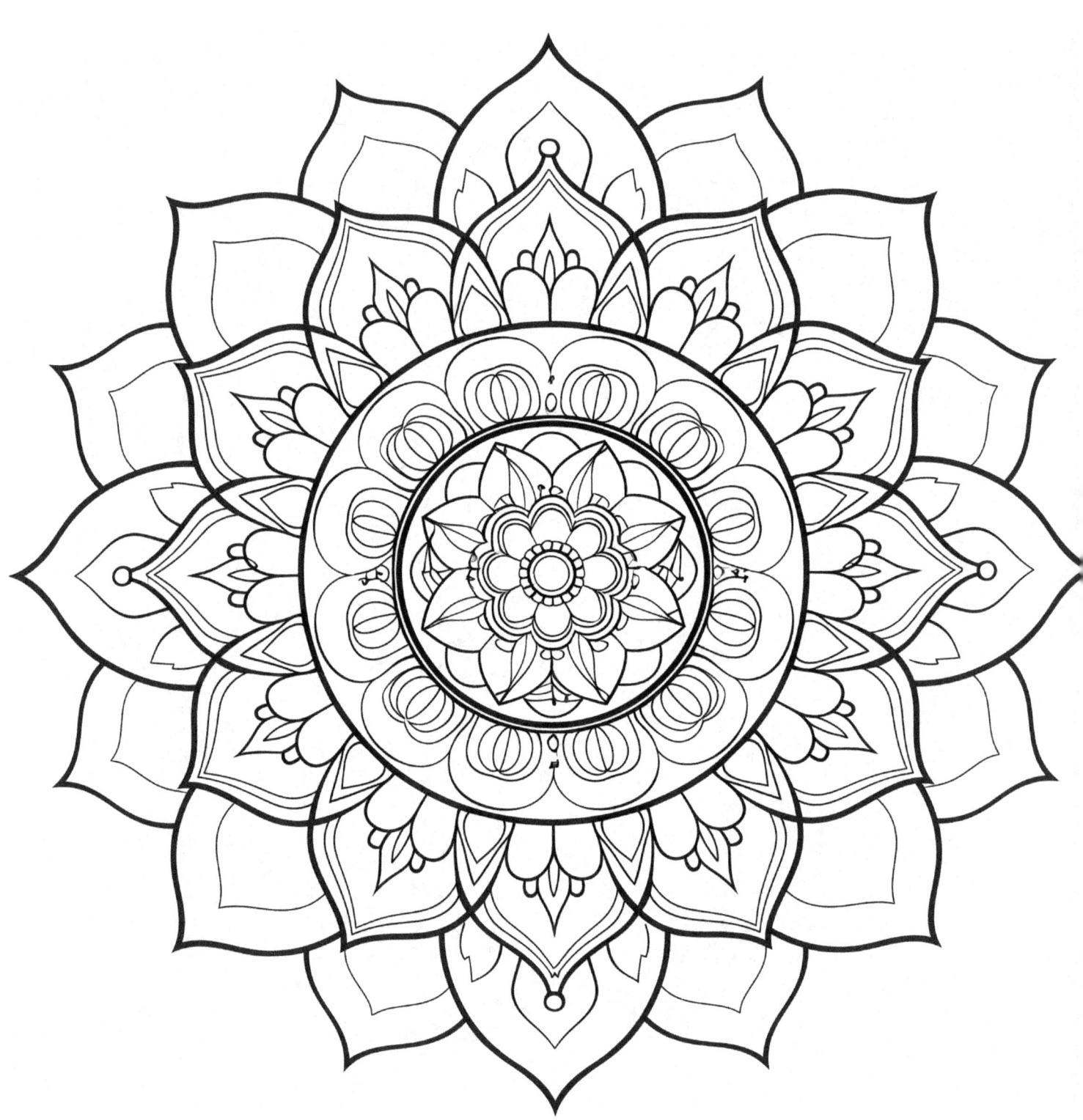

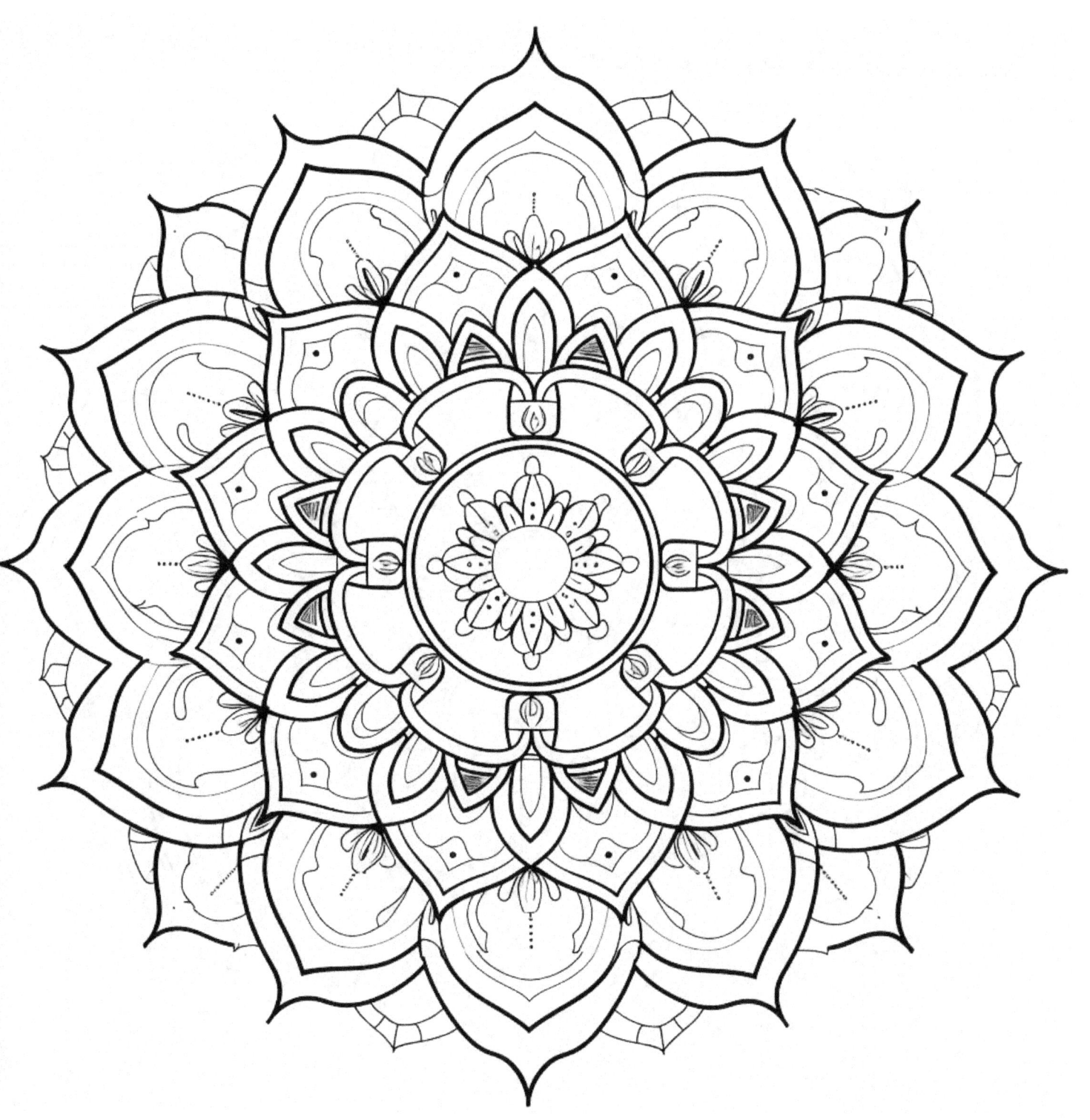

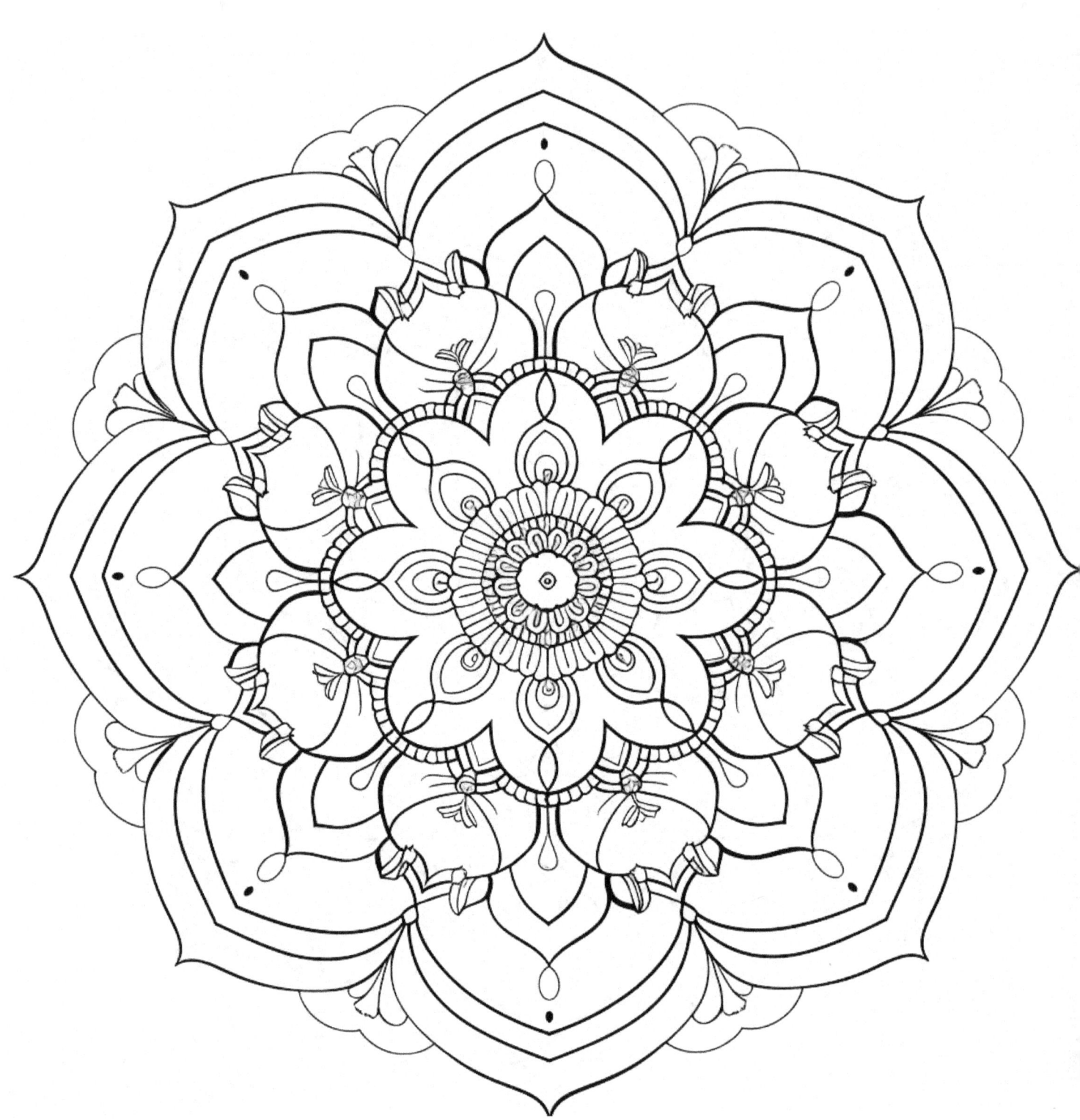

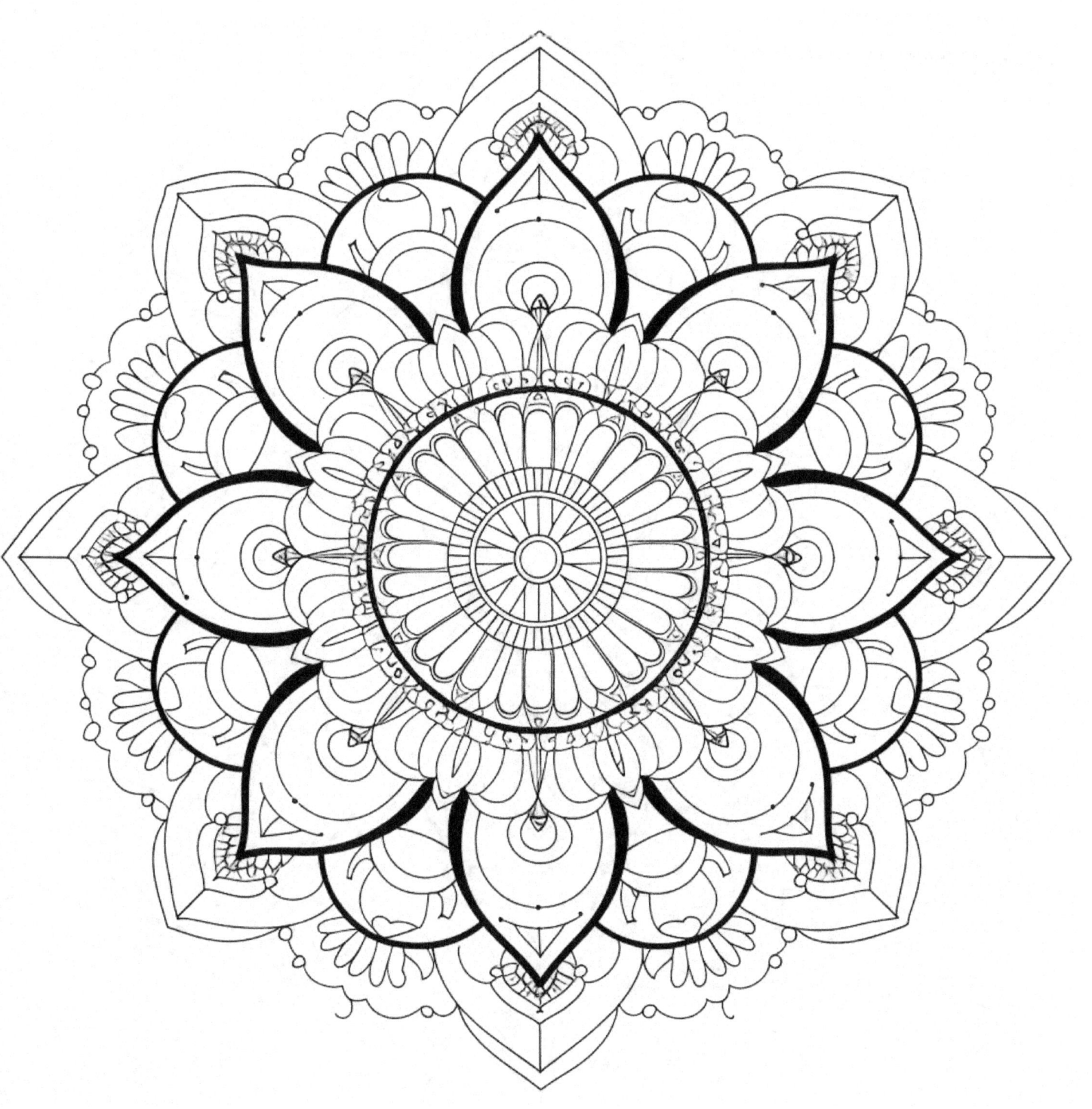

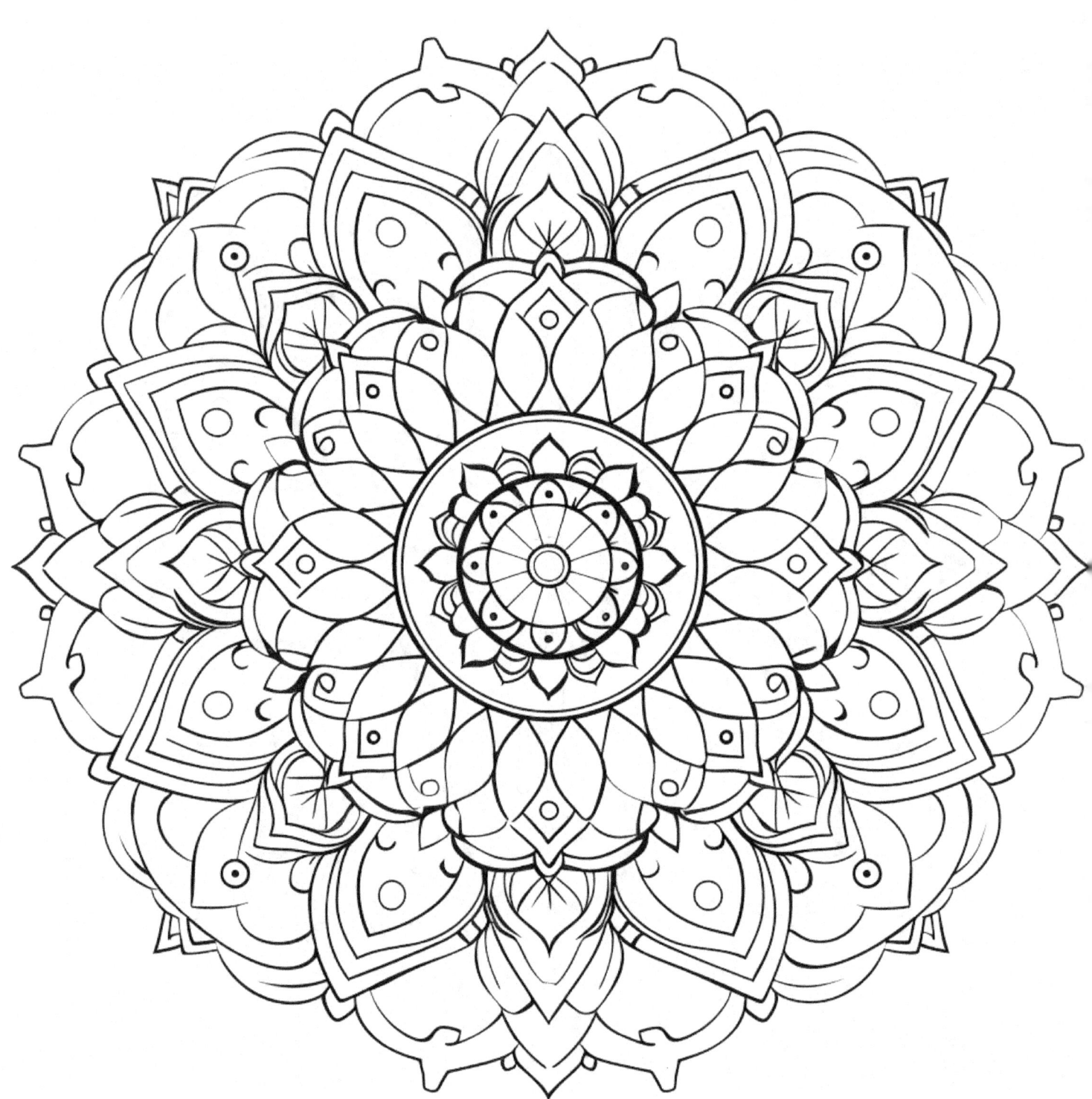

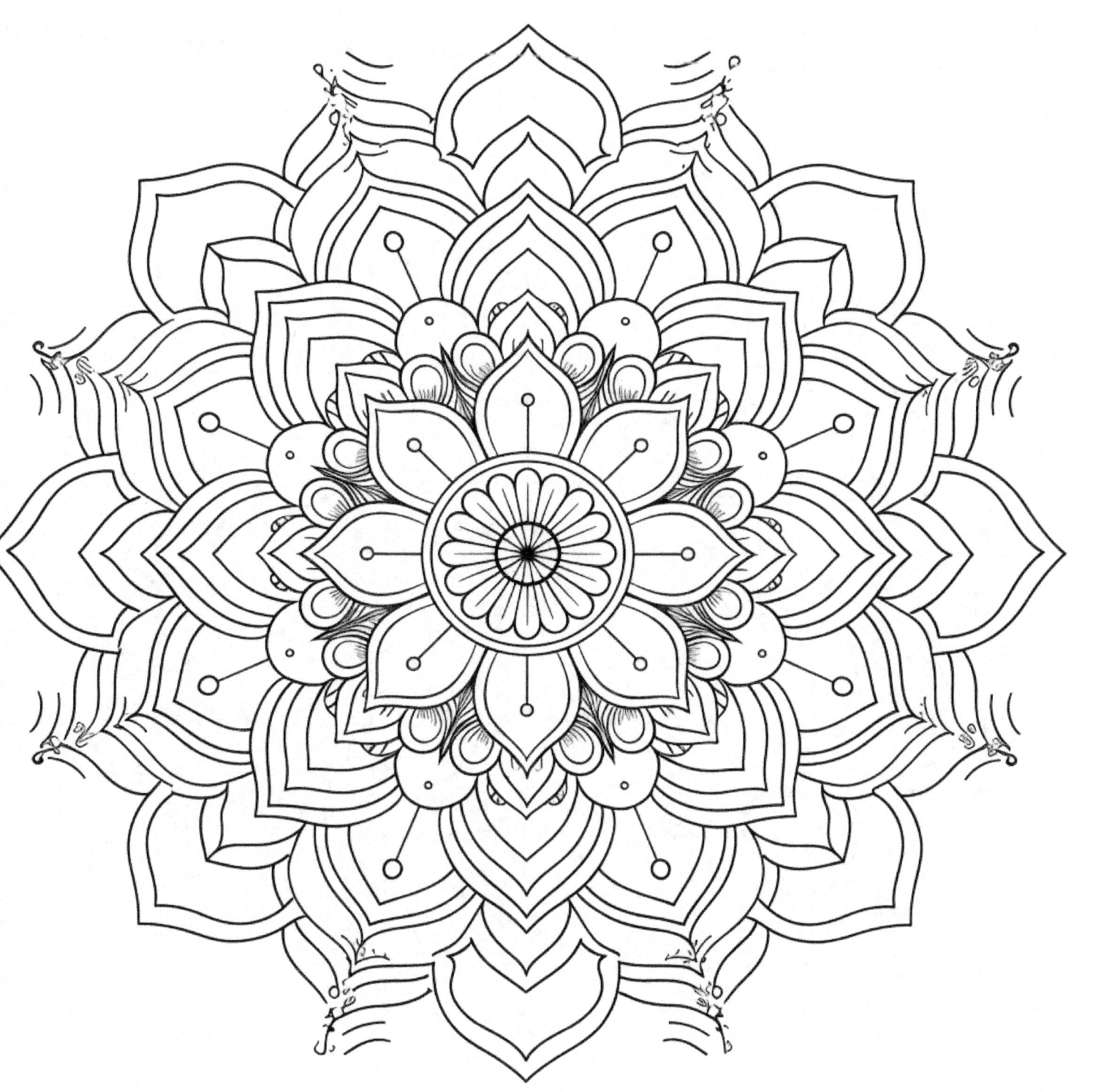

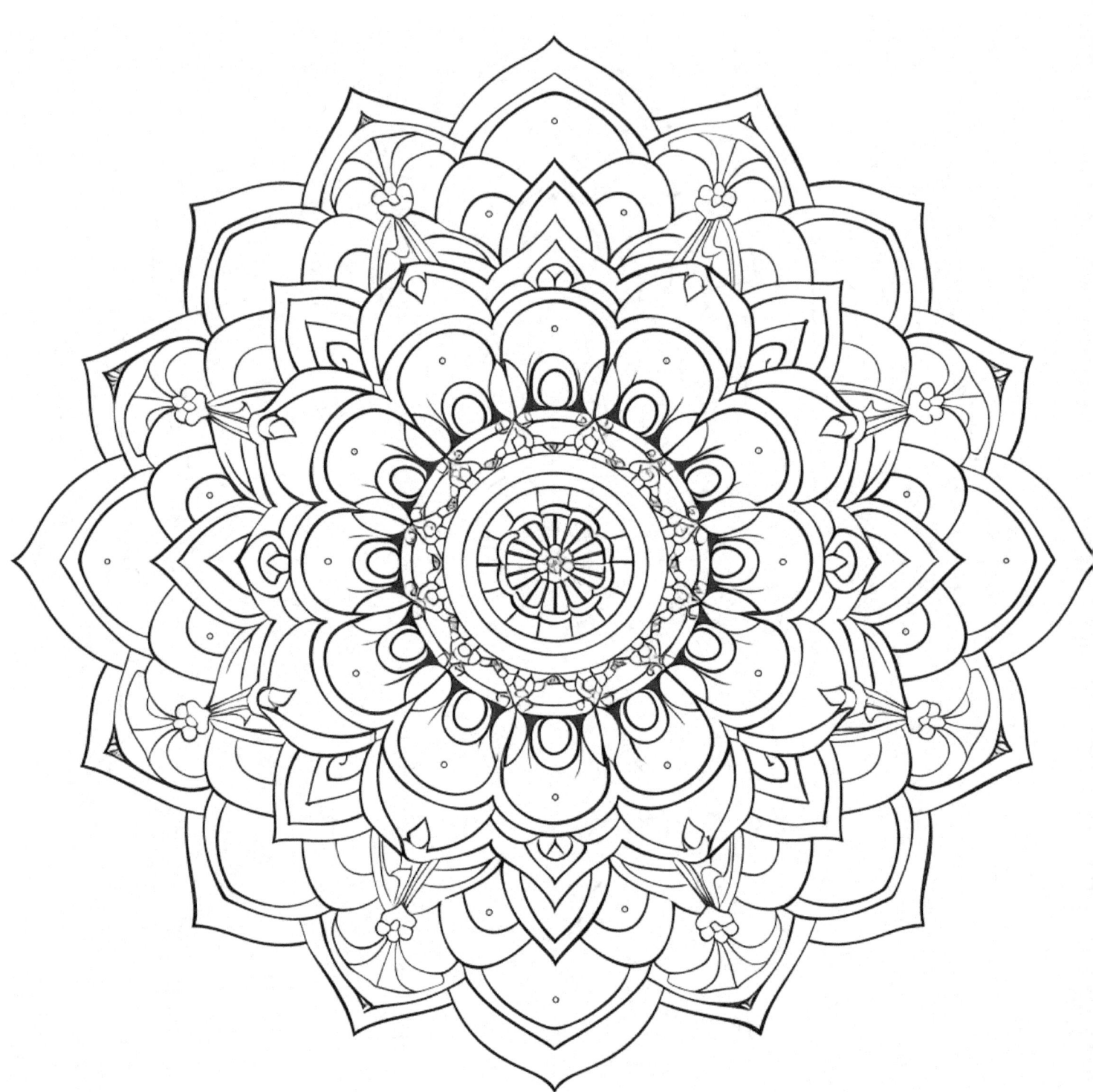

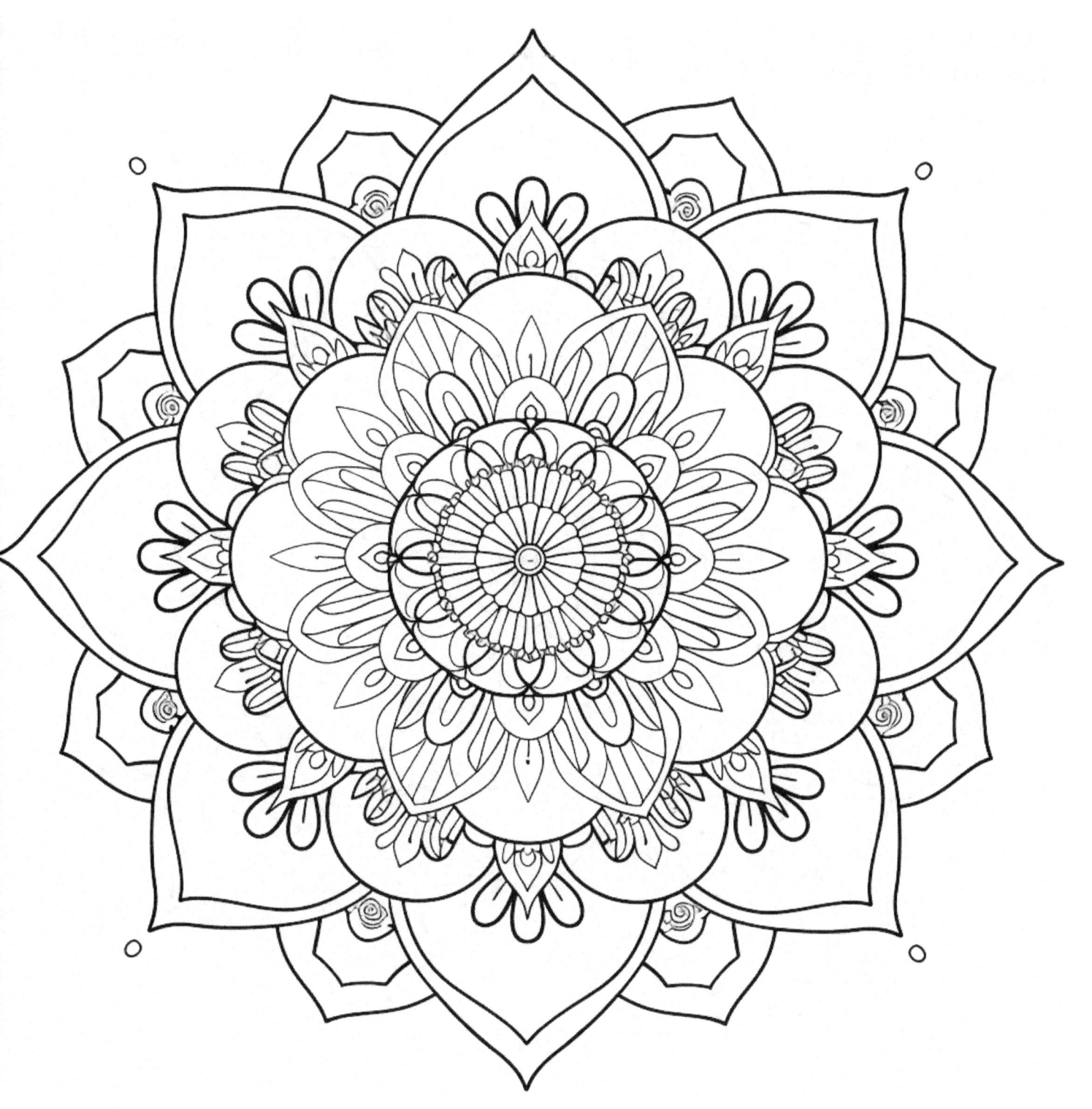

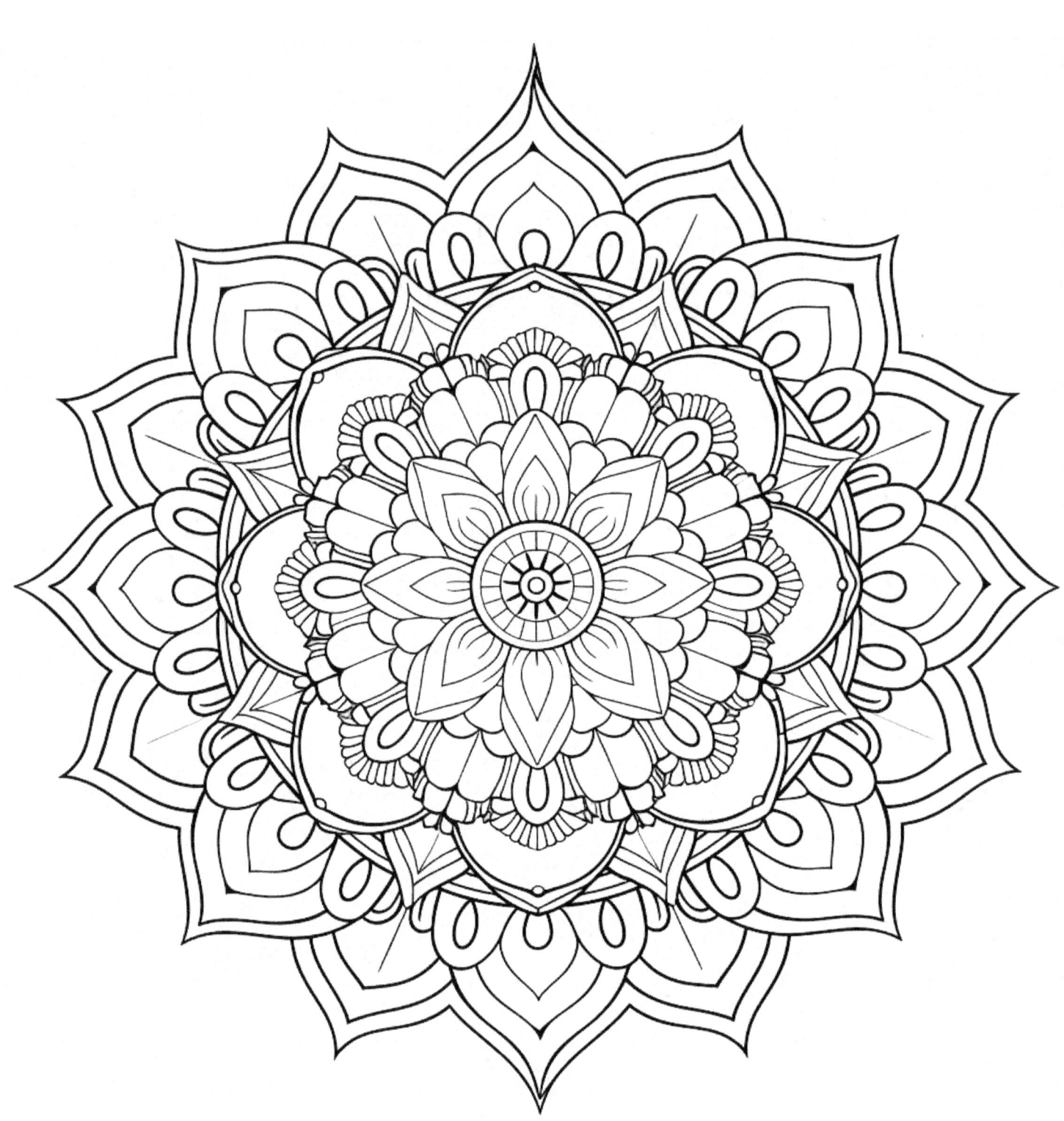

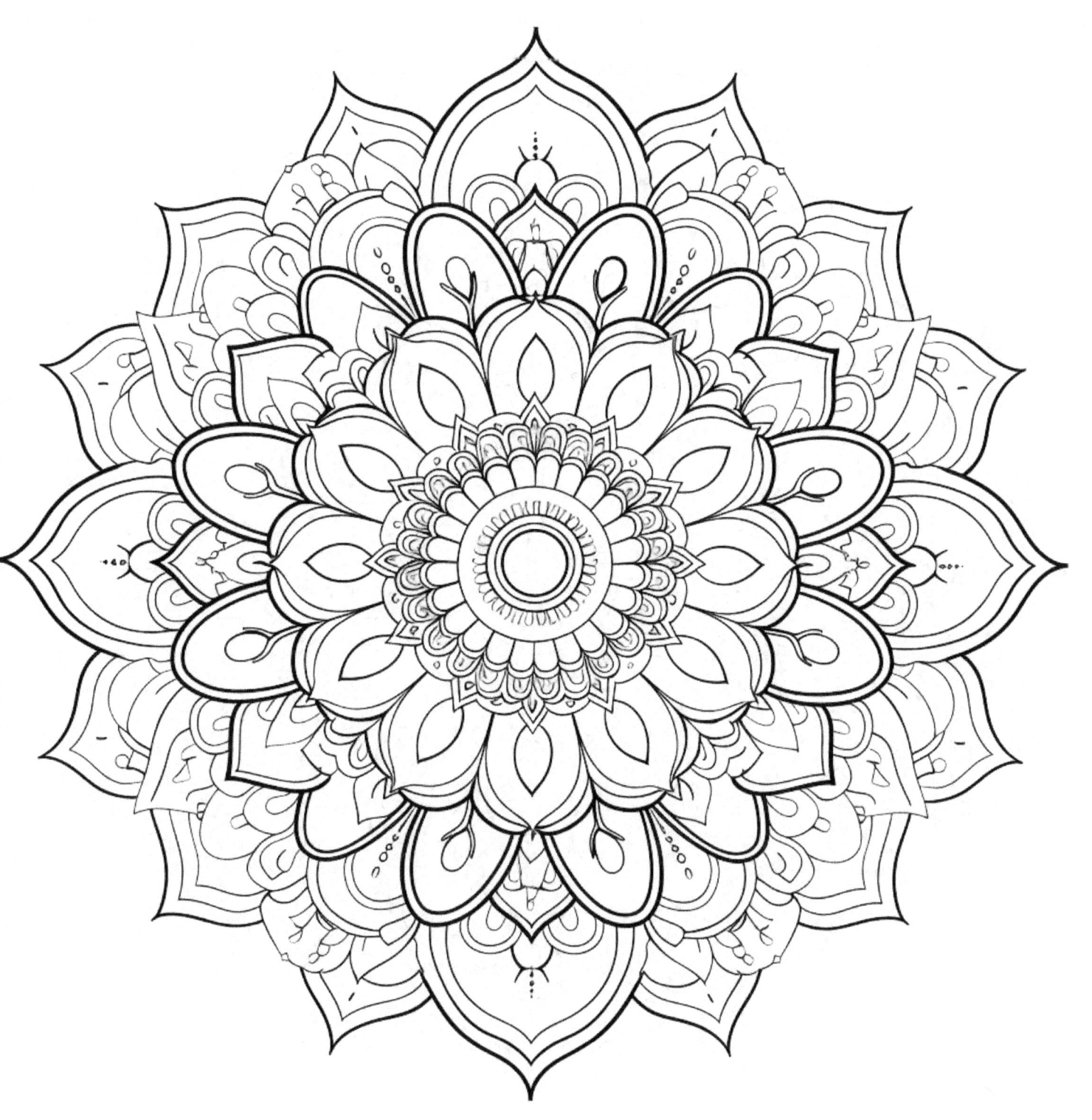

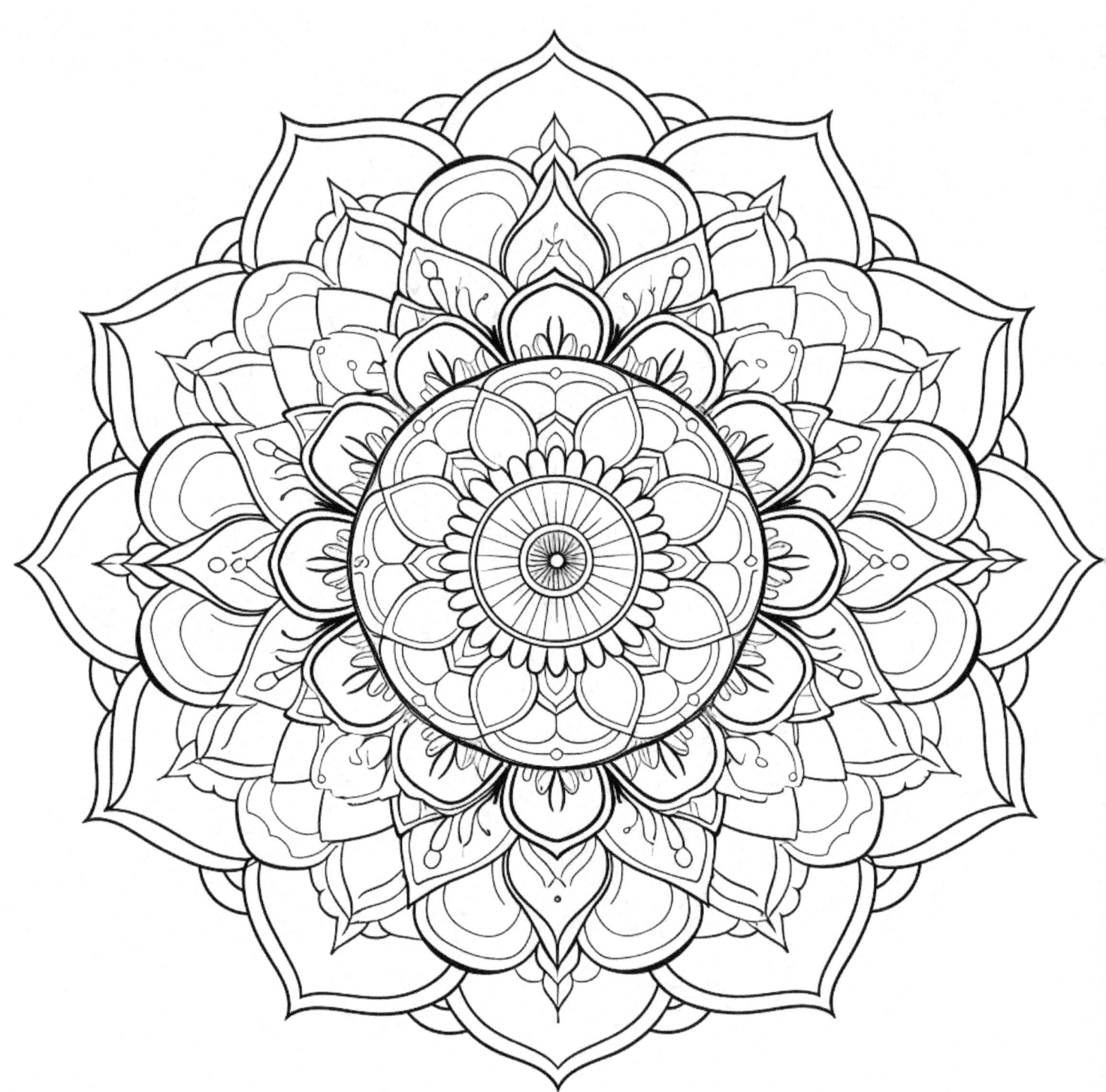

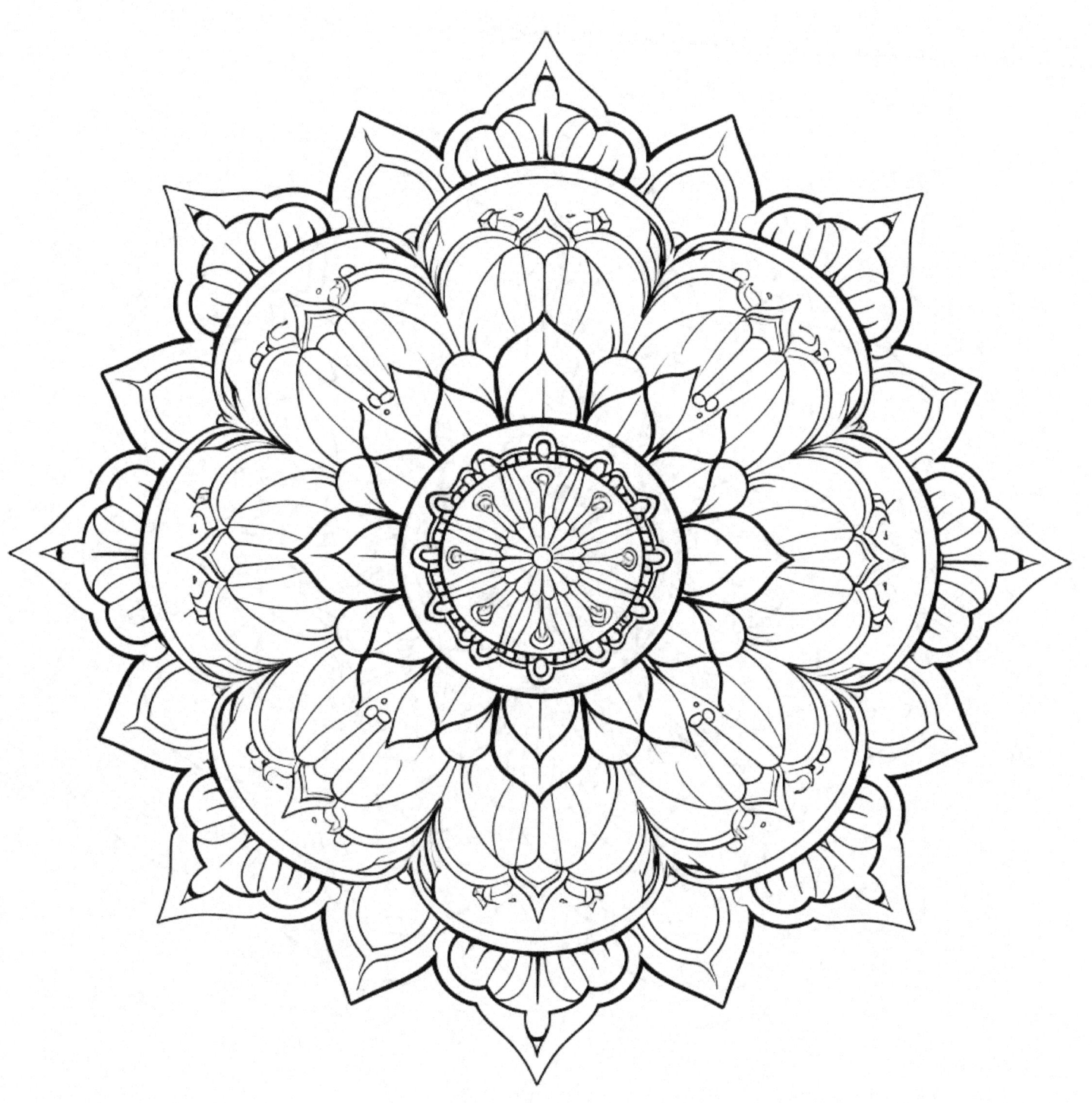

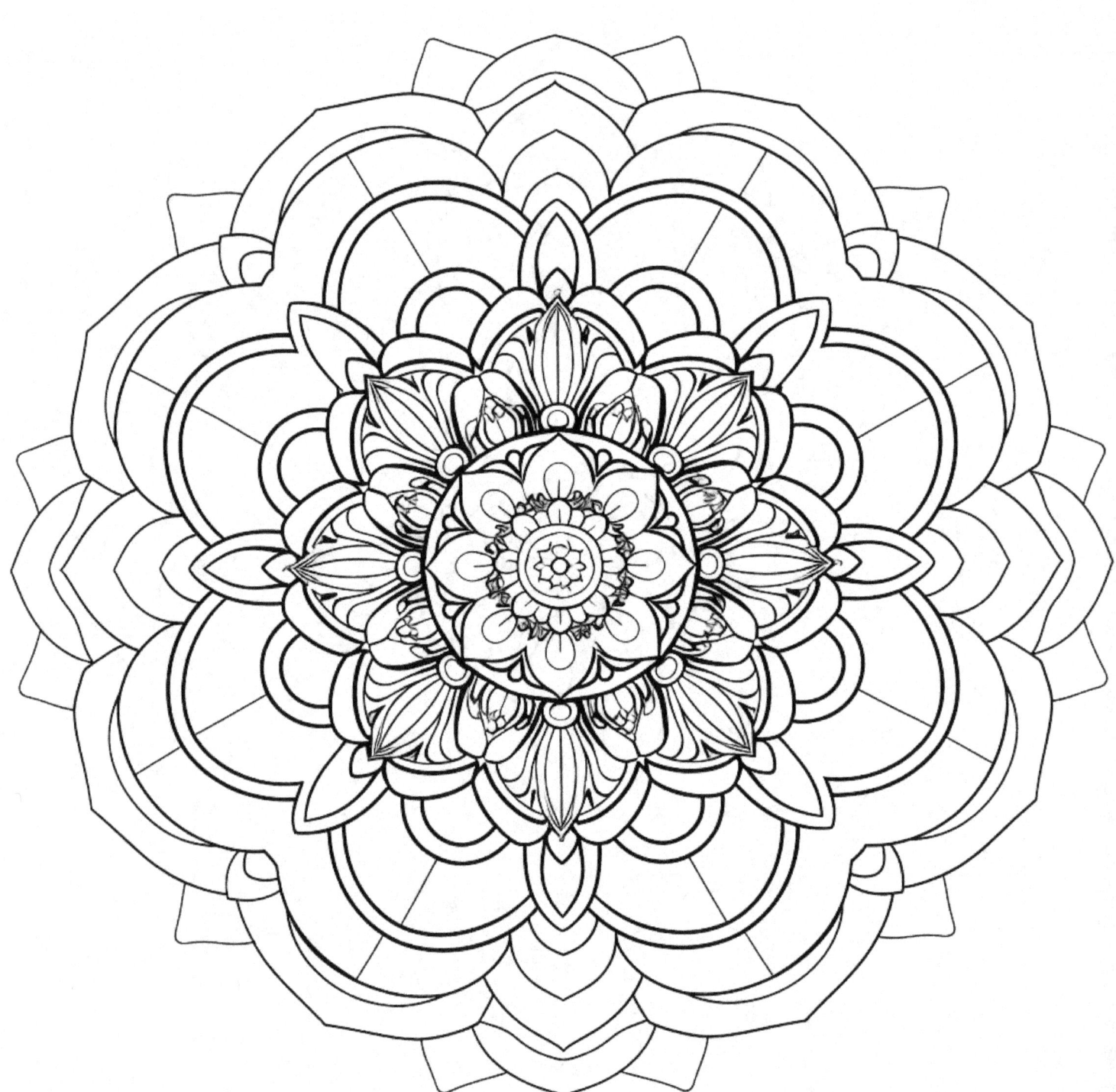

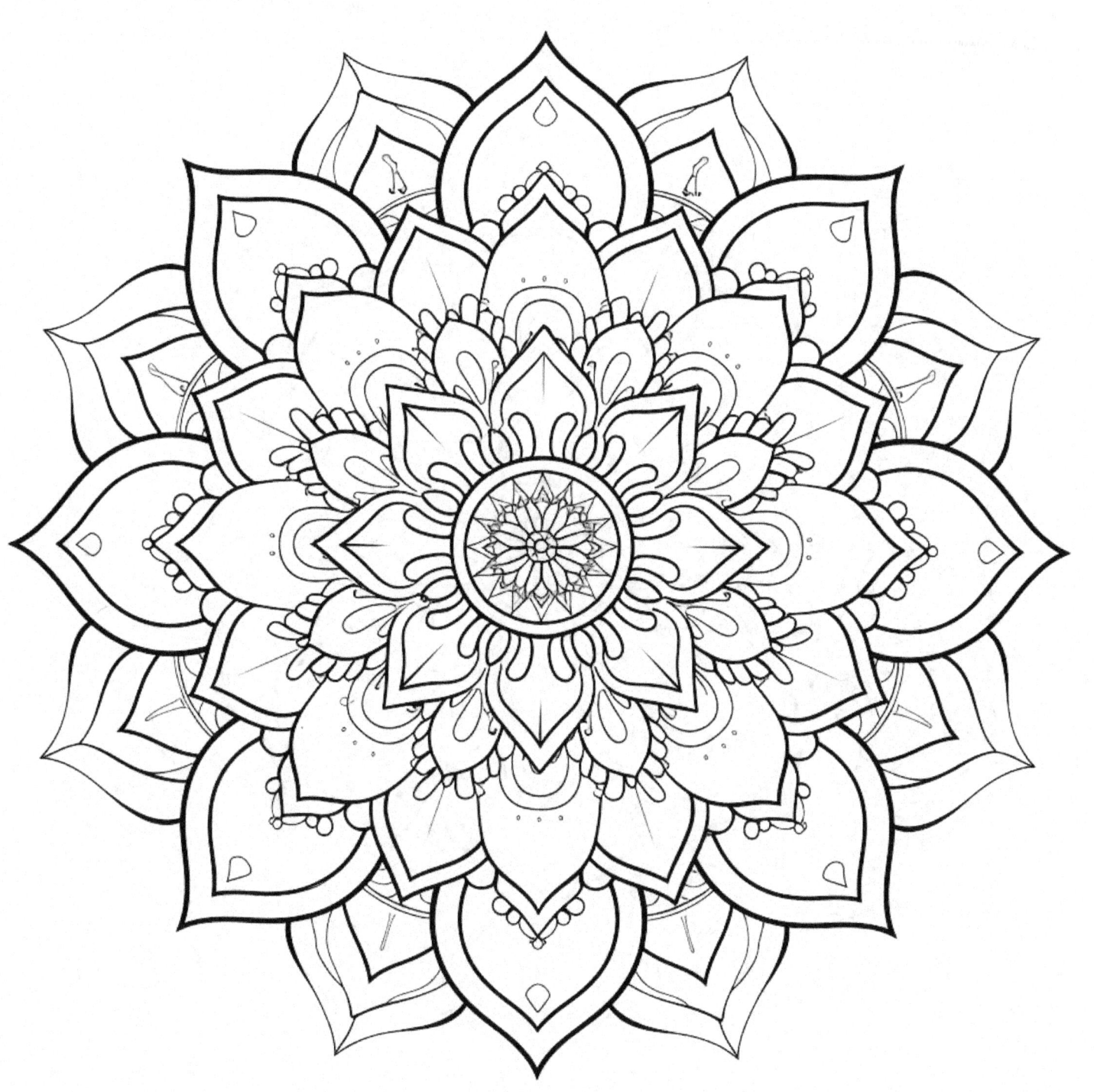

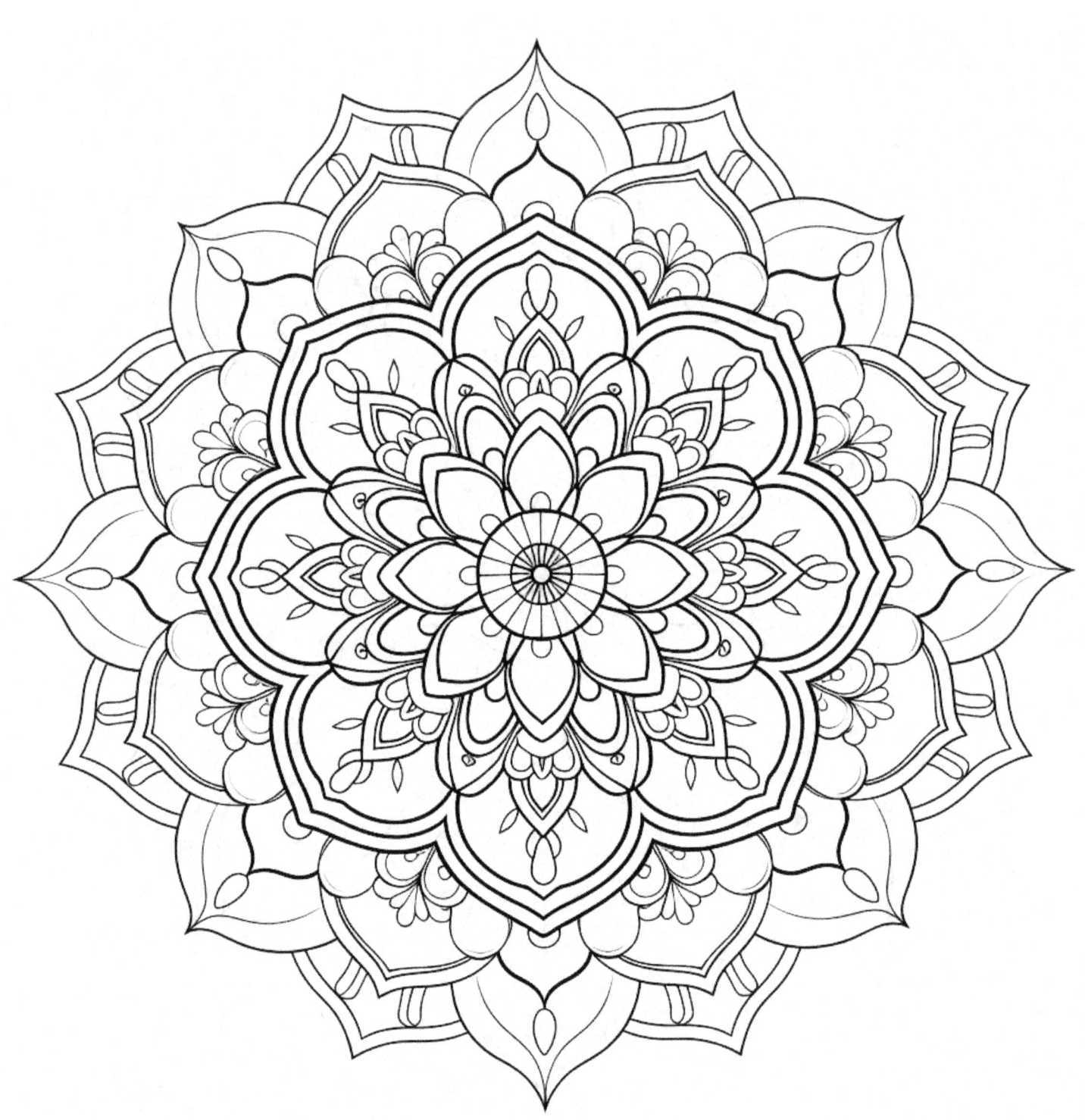

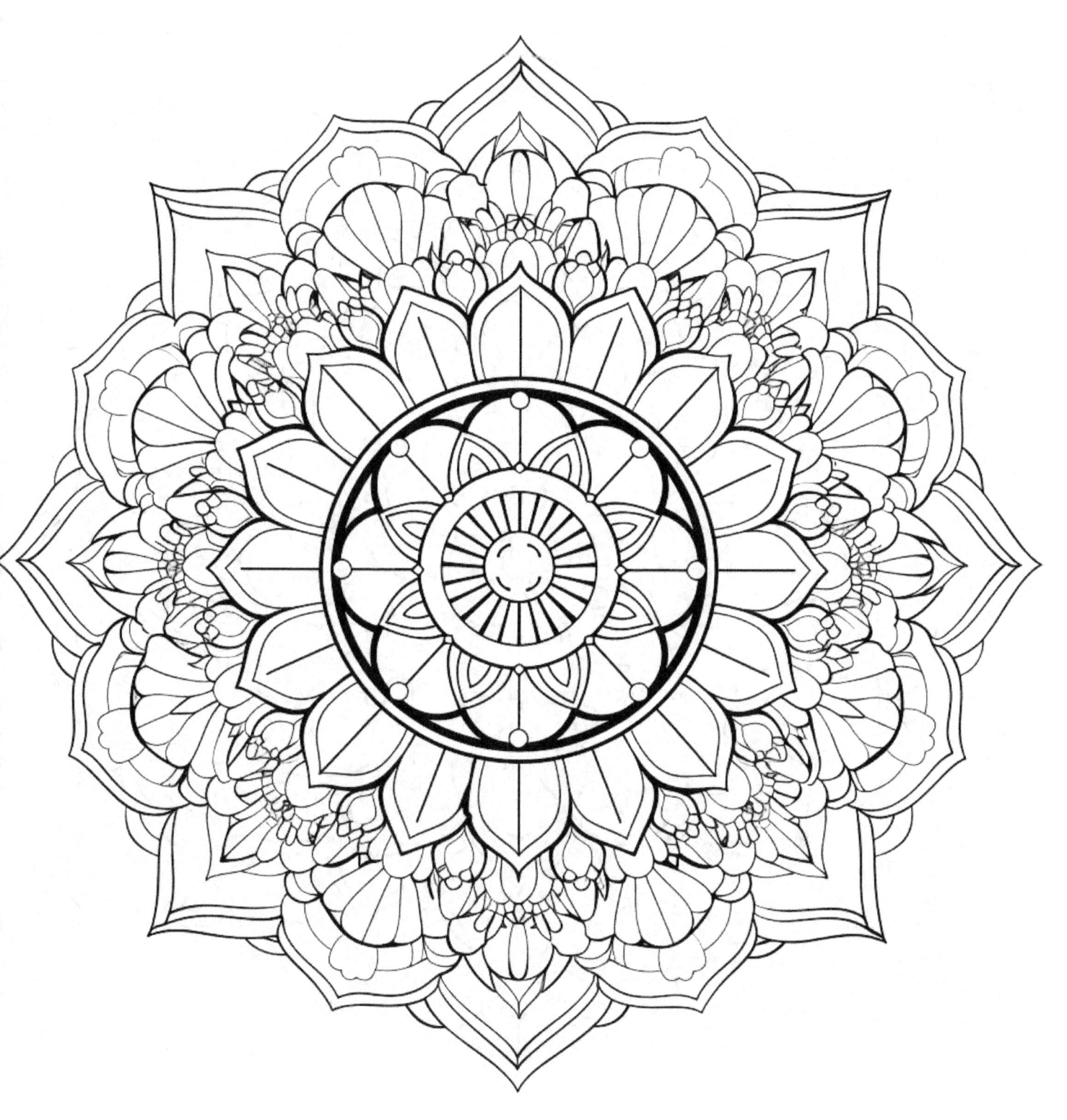

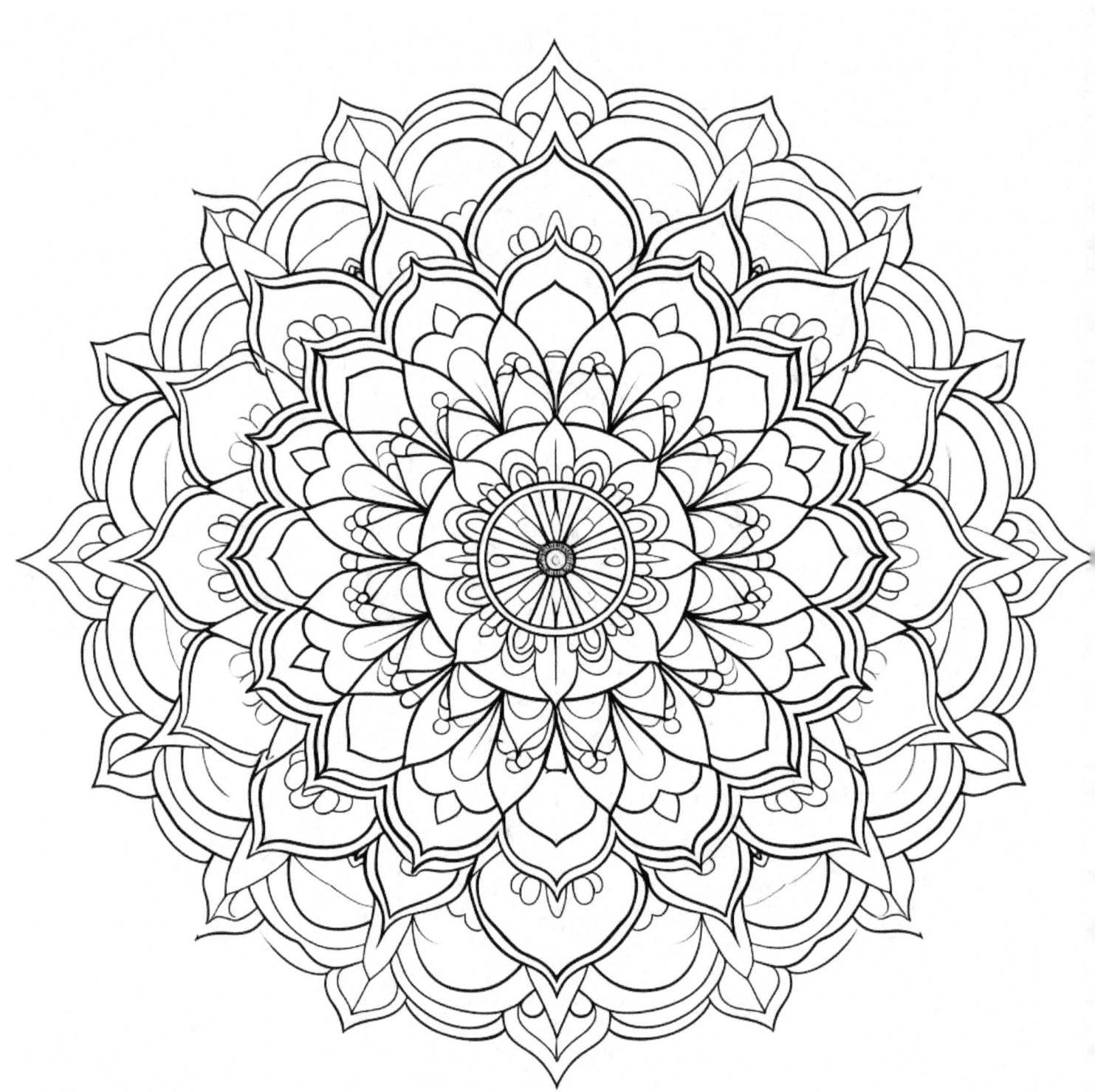

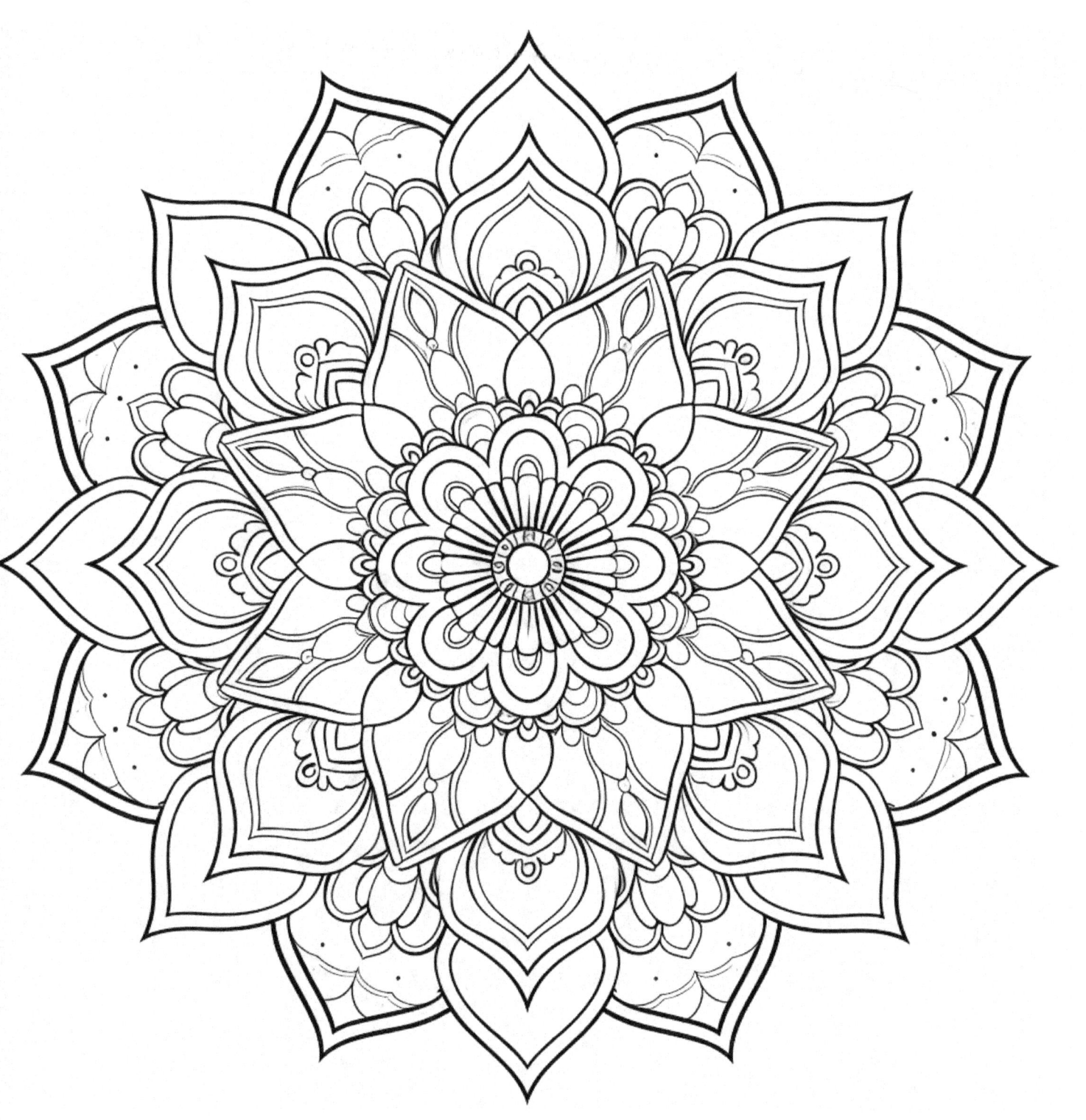

www.ingramcontent.com/pod-product-compliance
Lightning Source LLC
Chambersburg PA
CBHW062203220526
45470CB00009B/2905